THE SPIRIT OF YOUTH AND
THE CITY STREETS

THE
SPIRIT OF YOUTH
AND THE
CITY STREETS

by
JANE ADDAMS

With an Introduction by
ALLEN F. DAVIS

UNIVERSITY OF ILLINOIS PRESS
Urbana and Chicago

Illini Books edition, 1972

Introduction © 1972 by the Board of Trustees
of the University of Illinois
Manufactured in the United States of America
P   5   4   3   2

This book is printed on acid-free paper.

Library of Congress Catalog Card No. 72-76862
ISBN 0-252-00275-X

Originally published in 1909 by the Macmillan Company.

CONTENTS

INTRODUCTION

Allen F. Davis

Jane Addams always claimed that *The Spirit of Youth and the City Streets* was her favorite book. Published in 1909, it received praise from sociologists, psychologists, and other critics. William James wrote in the *American Journal of Sociology:*

> Certain pages of Miss Addams' book seem to me to contain immortal statements of the fact that the essential and perennial function of the Youth-period is to reaffirm authentically the value and the charm of Life. All the details of the little book flow from this central insight or persuasion. Of how they flow I can give no account, for the wholeness of Miss Addams' embrace of life is her own secret. She simply inhabits reality, and everything she says necessarily expresses its nature. She *can't help writing truth.*[1]

This was extravagant praise, but it was in no way unique, for in 1909 Jane Addams was probably the most famous

---

[1] *American Journal of Sociology* XV (Jan. 1910): 553. He said about the same thing in a letter to Jane Addams but added that it was "hard not to cry at certain pages." William James to Jane Addams, 13 Dec. 1909, Jane Addams Manuscripts, Swarthmore College Peace Collection.

woman in America. In that year she became the first woman to receive an honorary degree from Yale University and the first woman to be elected president of the National Conference on Charities and Corrections. Yet she was more than a celebrity; she was treated as a kind of spiritual leader, even a saint. One reviewer called her "The Lady Abbess of Chicago"; another said simply, "Miss Addams is a prophet. She brings us messages from God." But the review continued, "They are always messages for the time."[2] The last sentence was crucial, for Jane Addams was considered by many to be a special American kind of saint — practical, realistic, and useful, with special feminine insight into the problems of urban America. At a time when women were just beginning to take an active role in public life, she became the symbol of what woman could do. "Alert, a deep thinker, progressive, strong and tender-hearted, Jane Addams is a true type of useful American womanhood," *Leslie's Weekly* announced. Mrs. Ethelbert Stewart, wife of the labor leader and journalist, wrote, "I thank God for the intuitive motherhood that has made you see the needs so plainly, and the education and opportunity that has enabled you to express what you see, as we mothers of large families cannot."[3]

The legend of Jane Addams, which depicted her as a heroine and saint, influenced all those in her day who read what she wrote and continues to affect her reputation today.

[2] Harriet Park Thomas in *American Journal of Sociology* XV (Jan. 1910): 552-53; *New York Observer,* 16 Dec. 1909.

[3] *Leslie's Weekly,* 9 Dec. 1909; Mrs. Ethelbert Stewart to Jane Addams, Dec. 1909, Swarthmore College Peace Collection.

The legend is important in itself, but it obscures what she actually did. A careful reading of *The Spirit of Youth* may help separate the myth from the reality, but there are other reasons for a new edition at this time. *The Spirit of Youth* is certainly one of Jane Addams's best books. It establishes beyond doubt that she was a literary craftsman as well as a reformer. The book has been overshadowed by her autobiography, *Twenty Years at Hull House*, which appeared the next year, and her writing on peace, especially *The Newer Ideals of Peace* (1907) and *Peace and Bread in Time of War* (1922). Yet *Spirit of Youth* has much to tell us today; it offers perspective on youth culture, juvenile delinquency, drug addiction, the generation gap, the search for community in the city, and many other problems that still beset urban America. It is also an important book for understanding the emergence of concern for adolescence in the early twentieth century.

The concept of adolescence, of a time between childhood and adulthood, is such a commonly held assumption about the process of human development that it is accepted without thinking by most people today. Yet, as a number of scholars have recently pointed out, the idea of adolescence has had a relatively short history. The concept of a special time between childhood and adulthood developed gradually during the nineteenth century, but it was not until the first decade of the twentieth century that the idea became firmly planted in the national consciousness.[4]

---

[4] This and the following paragraphs depend heavily on Philippe Aries, *Centuries of Childhood: A Social History of Family Life,* tr.

In pre-industrial, rural societies there was usually no conception of children as a special group. They were seen as miniature adults. The boys were potential farmers or craftsmen, the girls potential mothers and homemakers. In Puritan Massachusetts a child seems to have been considered depraved and treated like an adult, dressed like an adult, and given adult tasks sometime between the ages of six and eight. The eighteenth and nineteenth centuries witnessed a developing concern for childhood as a special time of innocence and development, and gradually the concept of an intermediate period of storm and stress and preparation emerged. This change was tied closely to industrial and urban developments and to the movement of population into the cities. A farm family had a great deal of unity; adults and children shared the same work, entertainment, and friends. But a move to the city often caused the breakdown of the family as an economic unit. Children and adults were separated during the day, and adolescents had much more contact with others of their age group. At the same time new employment opportunities, and eventually state laws, re-

---

Robert Baldick (New York, 1962); John and Virginia Demos, "Adolescence in Historical Perspective," *Journal of Marriage and the Family* XXXI (Nov. 1969): 632-38; John Demos, *A Little Commonwealth: Family Life in Plymouth Colony* (New York, 1970); Bernard Wishy, *The Child and the Republic: The Dawn of Modern American Child Nurture* (Philadelphia, 1968). See also Joseph M. Hawes, *Children in Urban Society: Juvenile Delinquency in Nineteenth-Century America* (New York, 1971), and Joseph F. Kett, "Adolescence and Youth in Nineteenth-Century America," *Journal of Interdisciplinary History* II (Autumn, 1971), 283-98.

quired longer periods of schooling and the extension of childhood. There were class and ethnic distinctions and differences, of course, but industrial and urban changes affected all families to some extent and contributed to the discovery of childhood and adolescence.

After 1825 in the United States there was a great increase in the number of child-rearing books published; examples are Lydia M. Child's *The Mother's Book* (Boston, 1835) and H. W. Bulkeley's *A Word to Parents* (Philadelphia, 1858). These books decried the breakdown of parental authority and the increasing separation of young and old. Also published in greater numbers were books offering advice to adolescents (though the term generally used was "youth"). Such books as Henry Ward Beecher's *Lectures to Young Men* (Boston, 1844), Theodore Munger's *On the Threshold* (Boston, 1881), and Henrietta Keddie's *Papers for Thoughtful Girls* (Boston, 1860) had a wide sale. These books depicted youth as a critical transition period of life, a time when "passions" increased, when temptations had to be faced and overcome. Many writers associated these temptations and dangers with the corrupting influence of the city. Urban life as a corrupter of youth was also a favorite theme in the McGuffey Readers and in much of the popular fiction of the nineteenth century. In the 1890s books began to appear which dealt specifically with the problem of the slum child. Franklin H. Briggs in *Boys as They Are Made and How to Remake Them* (New York, 1894) blamed heredity for most delinquency. But Jacob Riis in *The Children of the Poor* (New York, 1892) argued that crowded tenements and filthy streets had something to do with juvenile crime in the city.

The point is that there was a considerable popular literature relating to youth and the city in the nineteenth century before there was any systematic attempt to study "youth" or adolescence. There was also, beginning in mid-century, a greater concern for "child study," stimulated by Darwin and especially by Friedrich Froebel and the kindergarten movement in Germany. The movement sought to develop the whole personality of the child, not through harsh discipline but, rather, through creative play and an introduction to art and music. In America the leader in the systematic child-study movement was G. Stanley Hall, a psychologist who after 1881 was president of Clark University. Hall's most influential work in this area, published in 1904, was *Adolescence: Its Psychology, and Its Relations to Physiology, Anthropology, Sociology, Sex, Crime and Education*. This encyclopedic work contained an immense amount of information and had a large impact on thinking about adolescence in many fields; indeed, it introduced the term "adolescence" into common usage. Perhaps his most important theory was his idea of "recapitulation," that a child in his growth and development "recapitulated" the history of the race, that babies in their need to grasp and small children in the urge to climb were showing their kinship with the apes. Adolescence in this theory took on a crucial importance, for it represented the most recent of man's great leaps, and the adolescent had the possibility of advancing beyond the present stage of civilization. But

Hall also saw this transitional stage as a troubled time of contradiction and emotional stress. Not everyone accepted Hall's ideas, and his theory of "recapitulation" was repudiated within two decades, but his work did serve to focus attention on the child and especially the adolescent.[5]

Jane Addams was familiar with Hall's work, and she used his theories in arguing for more parks and playgrounds for the children who needed an outlet for their animal energies. The romantic belief in the civilizing possibilities of youth that permeates *The Spirit of Youth* also owes something to Hall, as do constant references to primitive instincts. Yet she never once used the term "adolescence" in the book, preferring the older and more general word "youth." Her first thought was to call the book "Juvenile Delinquency and Public Morality" or "Juvenile Crime and Public Morals." She rejected these titles because they seemed too sociological, implying facts and figures and footnotes, and she had something more literary in mind, something that would appeal to a wide audience.[6]

Obviously Jane Addams was influenced by the writing of G. Stanley Hall and by the work of sociologists and other experts on adolescence and juvenile crime. But of greater importance were her observations in Chicago and the memories of her own childhood and youth. Part of her

[5] On Hall's ideas, see Lawrence A. Cremin, *The Transformation of the School: Progressivism in American Education, 1876-1957* (New York, 1961), pp. 101-4, and Nathan G. Hale, Jr., *Freud and the Americans: The Beginnings of Psychoanalysis in the United States, 1876-1917* (New York, 1971), pp. 100-109.

[6] Edward Marsh to Jane Addams, 23 Feb. 1909, Swarthmore College Peace Collection.

genius and success as a writer was her ability to adapt the theories of others and to make universal her own experience. Everything she wrote was in a real sense autobiographical.

Jane Addams grew up in Cedarville, Illinois, a small town near the Wisconsin border. She went to a one-room school, attended church and Sunday school, and roamed the hills and fields with her step-brother and the village children. They played chess, "King and Queen," and "crusades," or occasionally the girls watched the boys organize a sham battle or a parade. In winter they could slide down the gentle hills or skate on the mill pond. On special days, such as the Fourth of July, there were celebrations, and now and then a lecture, a revival meeting, or a wedding became a social occasion for young and old alike. Of course there were daily chores to do: cooking, cleaning, sewing, and needlework for the girls, feeding the cows and horses, splitting wood, and hoeing the garden for the boys. It was assumed by all in the village that girls were more domestic and more submissive than boys.

There was little sense of social class in Cedarville. Jane Addams, whose father owned the mill and several farms, as well as the largest house in town, played with the sons and daughters of the hired hands with little idea that she was superior. There was domestic help, of course, yet she learned how to sew and knit and bake bread. There was a sense of community in the small Illinois town, a close association between work and play, between young and old, between men and women of all backgrounds. Distinctions were made, but there was a feeling of belonging.

Cedarville was an important influence on Jane Addams.
Like a great many others of her generation, she left the
small town. She went away to college, she traveled twice
for extended periods in Europe, and eventually she moved
permanently to Chicago, but she always found time to visit
Cedarville, even in her busiest years. The memories of her
childhood became a reference point for evaluating and
understanding the massive changes taking place in America
during her own lifetime, and they enabled her to become
an interpreter of those changes.

In January 1889 Jane Addams and Ellen Starr, a college
classmate, moved to Chicago and began to talk about their
"scheme." They had a difficult time explaining that their
object was not to uplift the masses but to restore communi-
cations between the various parts of society, and that they
were going to live in the slums as much to help themselves
as to aid the poor. Some laughed at their idea, others
ignored them, but a surprisingly large number of men and
women rallied to their cause and offered assistance. They
quickly learned that they were not the first people in
America to have the idea of a settlement. Stanton Coit, also
influenced by Toynbee Hall, had established a settlement
in New York in 1886. In 1887 a group of Smith College
graduates organized College Settlement Association, which
founded a settlement in New York barely a week before
Miss Addams and Miss Starr moved into the dilapidated
mansion that would become Hull House. It was obvious
even before they began that they were a part of a national,
indeed an international, movement, and still they had only

the vaguest notion of what they would do once they had moved in. They knew they wanted to be neighbors to the poor, but beyond that they were not sure.

They furnished the house, put the pictures they had collected in Europe on the walls, and began doing what they knew best — teaching, lecturing, and explaining their art objects. Ellen Starr started a reading group to discuss George Eliot's *Romola,* and they organized art exhibits. One of their tasks, they firmly believed, was to bring an appreciation of beauty and art to those forced to live in the drab environment of the slums. But they soon discovered that the neighbors had more immediate concerns than art and literature. They needed better food, clothing, and housing. The cultural activities of Hull House remained important, but very quickly the settlement became involved in attempts to improve conditions in the neighborhood, the city, and the nation.[7]

From the beginning it was the plight of the children and the young people that depressed the settlement workers most. They opened a kindergarten, began clubs and classes for the older children, and established the first public playground in Chicago in 1893. They also became aware of the horrors of child labor. The sallow-cheeked youngster forced to work twelve hours a day in a factory, the stunted and deformed and crippled children in the neighborhood were

[7] See Allen F. Davis, *Spearheads for Reform: The Social Settlements and the Progressive Movement* (New York, 1967); and Allen F. Davis and Mary Lynn McCree, eds., *Eighty Years at Hull House* (Chicago, 1969), for the story of the growth and impact of Hull House.

constant reminders of the problem. But the campaign against child labor really began when Florence Kelley moved to Hull House at the end of 1891. A large and powerful woman, educated at Cornell and the University of Zurich, she was an expert social investigator and a socialist. More radical than Jane Addams and the other residents, she forced them to confront the working and living conditions in the city. As chief factory inspector for Illinois, a job she held for four years, she made careful studies documenting the extent of child labor in the area and then mobilized a campaign to pass a state law against the abuse.

Florence Kelley was only one of a remarkable group of talented women who made Hull House the vital institution it became. There was also Julia Lathrop, a graduate of Vassar, an executive with a sense of humor and a passion for research. Alzina Stevens, a former labor leader, and Mary Kenny, a vivacious Irish girl from the neighborhood who became a labor organizer for the American Federation of Labor, both participated. Later there were Alice Hamilton, a doctor who became an expert on industrial disease, Grace and Edith Abbott, two sisters from Nebraska who pioneered in working with immigrants and became leaders in a variety of reform movements, and many more. A number of wealthy and socially prominent Chicago women never became residents, but they gave their time and money to the settlement. Most important of these talented and dedicated women were Mary Rozet Smith, Jane Addams's long-time friend and constant companion, and Mrs. Louise deKoven Bowen, a strong-minded woman who donated several buildings at Hull House as well as the summer camp and who served as treasurer and trustee of the settlement.

There were men too: residents like Edward Burchard and George Hooker, as well as others who came for a few months or a few years, such as the historian Charles Beard, William Lyon Mackenzie King, the future prime minister of Canada, and Gerard Swope, who would one day be president of General Electric. Many others, some famous, others unknown, visited the settlement or dropped in for a meal or a lecture. Over it all presided Jane Addams, called "Miss Addams" by all but her closest friends and treated with awe and almost reverence by many of the residents. She was occasionally resented, even hated, but she had the ability to solve differences, calm disagreements, and engineer compromises. She was given credit in the press for all that was accomplished at Hull House when often it was someone else who was responsible for an innovation. But Jane Addams was the acknowledged leader, the publicist, the one who wrote the articles and the books, made the speeches, and related the activities in and around Hull House to broader conceptions and movements.

Jane Addams and the others at Hull House were constantly studying their neighborhood, discovering problems which led them to initiate reforms at the city, state, or national level. Their concern for playgrounds and the need for parks and recreation led them to promote recreation centers in the city and to participate in the national play movement. When the National Playground Association of America was formed in 1906, Jane Addams was on the executive com-

mittee. The Hull House residents' experiments with kinder-
gartens and adult education made them pioneers in progressive education. They tried to make the classroom relate
to the reality of the world, and they believed that the school
should be the center of the community. Their thinking
paralleled that of John Dewey, and for good reason. Dewey
was a good friend of the Hull House group, a frequent vis-
itor to the settlement, and a member of the board of trustees. He learned from Hull House as the settlement workers
learned from him.

Interest in young people in the neighborhood led the
settlement residents to begin many other programs. Jane
Addams was concerned with the widening split she observed
between the immigrants and their children. As the children
became Americanized, they tended to rebel against the
language, customs, religion, and even the clothes of their
mothers and fathers. In order to illustrate that the ways of
the old country were not useless, she encouraged festivals
and the preservation of native handicrafts, and in 1900 she
organized the Hull House Labor Museum. By employing
some of the older artisans as teachers, the Hull House reformers hoped to restore some of the immigrants' pride in
the heritage of the Old World while at the same time giving the younger generation an appreciation of that heritage.
They also believed that by showing the history of the textile
industry or the process by which wheat was made into
bread, or by teaching the ancient art of pottery making or
wood carving, that they could demonstrate the relationship
between raw material and finished product, a relationship

that had disappeared in the modern factory. They also hoped to restore a pride in workmanship and a respect for useful things of beauty. Unfortunately, it was often a forlorn hope and a romantic dream.

The Labor Museum, the clubs and classes, and other activities did not keep the young people who lived in the Hull House neighborhood from getting into trouble with the law. The settlement workers were disturbed that many juvenile offenders were picked up for minor offenses and then were thrown together with hardened criminals. The spirit of adventure, the impulsive action, that would be of little consequence for the rural youth often resulted in a prison term and a life of crime for the city youngster. Concerned about this situation, the Hull House group agitated for the new law that, in 1899, provided for the first juvenile court in the nation. The juvenile court was not a criminal court, and it was supposed to keep the rights and interests of the offender chiefly in mind. The judge could put the delinquent on probation, make him a ward of the state, or assign him to an institution. While the main idea was to help rather than to penalize the child, it did not always work out that way, for the judge had great power while the offender had none of the rights of due process. Not until 1967 did a U.S. Supreme Court decision recognize that even juvenile offenders were entitled to procedural rights. Still, at the time, the juvenile court represented a major breakthrough in the treatment of boys and girls in trouble. Alzina Stevens of Hull House was the first probation officer of the court, and Julia Lathrop and then Mrs. Bowen were successively chairwomen of the Juvenile Court Committee. Through the cases that came before the court the Hull House residents had a chance to study systematically the problem of the juvenile delinquent and to try to understand why he got into trouble with the law. Jane Addams used material collected by the juvenile court to illustrate *Spirit of Youth,* and she dedicated the book to Mrs. Bowen, the chairman of the court committee.

The tragedy and pathos of the young offenders who came before the juvenile court not only inspired Jane Addams's book but also stimulated further attempts to solve the problem of juvenile crime. In 1909, the same year that *The Spirit of Youth* was published, the Hull House reformers organized the Juvenile Protective Association, an outgrowth of the Juvenile Court Committee. One of its purposes was to control or eliminate poolrooms, bars, dance halls, theaters, and other institutions that the committee felt were breeders of crime and vice. Also in 1909 the reformers founded the Juvenile Psychopathic Institute at Hull House. Under the direction of Dr. William Healy, it became a leading center for research into the causes of delinquency. Healy's careful studies resulted in such books as *The Individual Delinquent* (1915), which rejected the theory that delinquency and crime were primarily caused by heredity. He emphasized that while delinquency had many causes, environment was the most important. In a more informal way, without the scientific evidence, Jane Addams came to a similar conclusion in her book.

Jane Addams wrote *The Spirit of Youth,* as she wrote

most of her books, by first approaching a topic in a speech, then reworking it into an article, and finally arranging and rewriting the articles into a book manuscript. She revised constantly. The first time she gave a speech she often spoke from notes, talking quietly and calmly with a voice that could be heard easily throughout the auditorium. She illustrated her points with stories of people, sometimes pathetic, occasionally heroic, but always believable. As she gave the speech again and again, the timing became better, the illustrations sharper, until gradually she developed a polished manuscript. Usually she wrote her material out by hand (a hand that became increasingly more difficult to decipher the busier she became) before giving it to a secretary to type. Then she would cut up the typed manuscript, putting it back together again with common pins while writing in transitions and new ideas.

Jane Addams thought of herself as a professional writer and took pride in her published work. "I have always liked to write," she told a reporter, "even as a girl in school. Later when I spent a few months in Europe I took great interest in the expressive arts. I have had this feeling in everything I have written; I have not written as a philanthropist merely."[8] Her articles appeared in a great variety of magazines, and often the same basic article appeared in several different places. She asked no fee from such journals as *Charities and the Commons* or *The Public,* but from the *Ladies' Home Journal* or *McClure's* she could drive a hard bargain.

[8] *New York Sun,* 30 Apr. 1910.

She also drove a hard bargain when it came to signing a book contract. Her books were published by the Macmillan Company, in large part because Richard T. Ely, economist, professor at the University of Wisconsin, and academic entrepreneur, had persuaded her to do a book for a series he was editing for Macmillan called the Citizen's Library. The book turned out to be *Democracy and Social Ethics,* published in 1902. Her next book, *The Newer Ideals of Peace,* appeared in the same series in 1907. As her reputation spread, Edward Marsh, the Macmillan editor, realized what a valuable property he had, and he gently prodded her through friendly letters to work on another book. His efforts paid off; in February 1909 she wrote suggesting she might have a manuscript on juvenile delinquency ready by 15 October. Marsh was delighted and offered her "a royalty of 13% on the retail price of the first 1500 copies sold and 15% on all copies sold thereafter." Jane Addams replied quickly:

> The terms you suggest are not as advantageous as those your company gave me for *Newer Ideals of Peace*. I have just looked over your account rendered April 30th, 1908, and find that I received 16¼ per cent upon 1112 copies of *Newer Ideals of Peace* and 16¼ per cent upon 497 of *Democracy and Social Ethics,* I am not able at this moment to lay my hand upon the original agreement, but I remember being paid an out and out sum when the manuscript was delivered. I think the sum was $100.[9]

As it turned out, she had confused 16¼ cents per copy with

[9] Marsh to Addams, 15, 23 Feb. 1909; Addams to Marsh, 25 Feb. 1909, Swarthmore College Peace Collection.

the percentage, which had been 13 on the previous books, but this penchant for bargaining for every dollar, for getting the best possible contract, was very much a part of her personality.

A determined pride and high professional standards motivated her as she prepared the book. It was to be composed of essays and speeches she had done over a period of two years, a speech before the National Society for the Promotion of Industrial Education, an article that had appeared in *Charities and the Commons* called "Public Recreation and Social Morality," an address given for the New York Playground Association, an article that had been published in the *Ladies' Home Journal* called "Why Girls Go Wrong," and some other material. In the spring and summer of 1909 she spliced the pieces together, rearranging and rewriting until she had a finished manuscript — a manuscript that, unlike some of her other work, was changed very little as it passed from typescript to galley proof to page proof. The book was published in November 1909 with two excerpts appearing in the *Ladies' Home Journal* in October and November. The Macmillan editor was not sure he liked the title of the book and was worried about confusion of copyright arising from the magazine excerpts and the book coming out so closely together, but he did appreciate the speed and efficiency with which Jane Addams worked. It had been barely nine months since she had suggested that she might have a manuscript ready for fall. Yet she could still write to a friend, "I am sending you a copy of the book which I regard with mixed emotions, one is gratitude that it is out at last, and the other regret that I did not fuss with it longer."[10]

The book was received with immediate enthusiasm. Professional reviewers, friends, sociologists, settlement workers, ministers, and ordinary citizens showered the book with praise, not only for its content but also for its literary style. And the book sold — 7,000 copies during the first year and a total of 18,000-20,000 during Jane Addams's lifetime — and many more got the message through her speeches and articles. One of the reasons for the success of the book, aside from the fact that Jane Addams wrote it, was its calm, optimistic answer to the problem of juvenile delinquency. She praised the exuberance, the energy, the good intentions, the creative possibilities of young people, and argued that it was only necessary to channel this creative force in the right direction.

Perhaps the most remarkable aspect of the book, given the time that it was written, was Jane Addams's appreciation of the importance of sex and the basic erotic instincts, although she did assume that the sex drive is more important for the male than for the female. She referred to "the emotional force," the "fundamental instinct," "this sex susceptibility." Although she knew nothing of Freud, she suggested that the sex drive furnished "the momentum toward all art." She argued that this natural instinct, if repressed, served as "a cancer in the very tissues of society" and resulted in all kinds of deviant behavior. A good por-

[10] Jane Addams to Julia Lathrop, n.d., 1909, Swarthmore College Peace Collection.

tion of the book is taken up with descriptions of how the modern city overstimulates the adolescent. "The newly awakened senses are appealed to by all that is gaudy and sensual, by flippant street music, the highly colored theater posters, the trashy love stories, the feathered hats, the cheap heroics of the revolvers displayed in the pawnshop windows," as well as movie theaters, dance halls, prostitution, and drugs.

The rural youth of another age, and of her memory, never had to face these temptations. In rural America the quest for adventure led to harmless pranks, but in the city the same impulse resulted in arrest and jail. She never argued for turning the clock back, for returning to the world of the small town, but rather she insisted on the need to channel and sublimate the natural drives of youth into creative and socially acceptable paths. She suggested Molière and Shakespeare to replace the cheap movie, chaperoned parties to compete with the dance halls, recreation centers and settlements to substitute for the saloon, parks and playgrounds and competitive sports to replace the spirit of adventure associated with drugs and liquor. She realized how difficult it was to find a "moral equivalent" for juvenile deliquency, and yet she revealed a certain naïve optimism in believing that her substitute would work. She is much more convincing in describing the irresistible attraction of the train, the movies, and the dance halls than in defining the alternatives. There is an assumption throughout that the lower-class urban environment of saloons, dance halls, and street life needed to be changed and made more like a middle- or upper-class neighborhood. And yet the book is amazingly free of moral superiority and puritanical preaching.

There was, however, another and more fundamental cause for the discontent of youth in the city — the industrial system which employed them for long hours in meaningless jobs. The city youth was not able to expend his energy in a worthwhile job as the rural youth could, for factory work tired only the nerves and the senses, not the body. Jane Addams understood the dullness and monotony of factory work, but her solutions seem to beg the question. She accepted the industrial revolution and realized that the machine was here to stay, but she had no great faith in technology. She wanted to control the machine so that it would not destroy the man who was forced to run it. She also wanted to preserve the art and skill of the craftsman. She put great faith in a practical industrial education to train young men and women for the real jobs they would be doing. She argued for a team spirit (for a kind of giant Labor Museum), so that thirty-nine men all working on the same product would appreciate that they were actually a meaningful part of one operation. She supported a revolt against shoddy, poorly designed products and against dehumanizing working conditions. But never did she carry her arguments to their logical conclusion and suggest that there was something fundamentally wrong with the industrial system. In the end, although she carefully documented the destruction being wrought by the factory, the best she could offer was to help adjust young people to the system and make them a little happier in the process.

Jane Addams sent a copy of her book to Vida Scudder, a Christian Socialist, an English professor at Wellesley College, and one of the founders of the College Settlement Association. After praising the "rare and lovely tenderness" of the book, Miss Scudder continued, "I rebuke myself, but I grow heavy of heart as the years pass on, 'save the children,' was our cry when the settlements started twenty years ago. Those children are men and women now, fathers and mothers and still we raise the same cry and hold the new generation under the same stupid and criminal conditions as the old. How long, O Lord how long?"[11] But Jane Addams, like most of the progressives, was more optimistic; unlike the socialists, she still had faith that the system could be patched up and made to work, that the right legislation would solve the difficulties. At the end of the book she poses the alternatives: "We may either smother the divine fire of youth or we may feed it. We may either stand stupidly staring as it sinks into a murky fire of crime and flares into the intermittent blaze of folly or we may tend it into a lambent flame with power to make clean and bright our dingy city streets." In 1972 the city's streets are still dingy, and another generation is held "under the same stupid and criminal conditions as the old." It is easy now to reject the opti-

[11] Vida Scudder to Jane Addams, 13 Nov. 1909, Swarthmore College Peace Collection.

mism of Jane Addams and echo the cry of Vida Scudder, "How long, O Lord how long?"

Yet as one reads *The Spirit of Youth,* despite its romantic optimism and its occasional archaic language, one is struck by the contemporary relevance of the book. Jane Addams used "colored" rather than "black," but already in 1909 she appreciated the need for the black youngster to search for his identity in an African past. Her discussion of the drug problem sounds as if it were written yesterday. She had little faith that the machine and technology would solve America's problems, as some did in her time. She occasionally betrayed the concern for racial differences that fascinated her generation, but she avoided seeing in those differences the cause of delinquency, as Jacob Riis and others did. She referred constantly to "primitive instincts" and the "primitive spirit of adventure," but she rejected the theory of Cesare Lombroso, still popular in 1909, that the criminal is an "atavistic reversal" or throwback to a more primitive form of man. Indeed, she rejected all versions of the hereditary explanation for delinquency and emphasized the child's relation to his environment, his family, and his neighborhood, while many experts in her day were finding the cause of delinquency in race, body type, or mental deficiency.

Jane Addams did not design the elaborate theory of growth and development that has characterized the work of Erik Erikson, but she does describe young people going through an "identity crisis." She appreciated the alienation and disaffection of the young in an urban and industrial world where there is little chance for a meaningful job or sense of community, and she would have agreed with many of the points made by Paul Goodman in *Growing Up Absurd*. Although by "youth" Jane Addams meant the time of life that Kenneth Keniston calls adolescence, rather than a post-adolescent period that is the product of a post-industrial age, she would agree with him that "it is a time of turmoil, fluctuations, and experimentation, when passing moods and enthusiasms follow each other with dizzying speed. The adolescent has little lasting sense of solidarity with others or with a tradition, and little ability to repudiate people and ideas that are foreign to his commitments."[12] Most of all, Jane Addams shares with Erikson, Keniston, and Goodman a faith in the potential, in the civilizing and regenerative power of the young — that more than anything else permeates every page of her book.

[12] The quotation is from Kenneth Keniston, *Young Radicals: Notes on Committed Youth* (New York, 1969). For Erikson, see especially *Childhood and Society* (New York, 1950) and *Identity, Youth and Crisis* (New York, 1968).

CHAPTER I
YOUTH IN THE CITY

CHAPTER I

YOUTH IN THE CITY

Nothing is more certain than that each generation longs for a reassurance as to the value and charm of life, and is secretly afraid lest it lose its sense of the youth of the earth. This is doubtless one reason why it so passionately cherishes its poets and artists who have been able to explore for themselves and to reveal to others the perpetual springs of life's self-renewal.

And yet the average man cannot obtain this desired reassurance through literature, nor yet through glimpses of earth and sky. It can come to him only through the chance embodiment of joy and youth which life itself may throw in his way. It is doubtless true that for the mass of men the message is never so unchallenged and so invincible as when embodied in youth itself. One generation after another has depended upon its young to equip it with gaiety and enthusiasm, to persuade it that living is a pleasure, until men everywhere have anxiously provided channels through which this wine of life might flow, and be preserved for their delight. The classical city promoted play with careful solicitude, building the theater and stadium as it built the market place and the temple. The Greeks held their games so integral a part of religion and patriotism that they came to expect from their poets the highest utterances at the very moments when the sense of pleasure released the national life. In the medieval city the knights held their tourneys, the guilds their pageants, the people their dances, and the church made festival for its most cherished saints with gay street processions, and presented a drama in which no less a theme than the history of creation became a matter of thrilling interest. Only in the modern city have men concluded that it is no longer necessary for the municipality to provide for the insatiable desire for play. In so far as they have acted upon this conclusion, they have entered upon a most difficult and dangerous experiment; and this at the very moment when the city has become distinctly industrial, and daily labor is continually more monotonous and sub-divided. We forget how new the modern city is, and how short the span of time in which we have assumed that we can eliminate public provision for recreation.

A further difficulty lies in the fact that this industrialism has gathered together multitudes of eager young creatures from all quarters of the earth as a labor supply for the countless factories and workshops, upon which the pres-ent industrial city is based. Never before in civilization have such numbers of young girls been suddenly released from the protection of the home and permitted to walk unattended upon city streets and to work under alien roofs; for the first time they are being prized more for their labor power than for their innocence, their tender beauty, their ephemeral gaiety. Society cares more for the products they manufacture than for their immemorial ability to reaffirm the charm of existence. Never before have such numbers of young boys earned money independently of the family life, and felt themselves free to spend it as they choose in the midst of vice deliberately disguised as pleasure.

This stupid experiment of organizing work and failing to organize play has, of course, brought about a fine revenge. The love of pleasure will not be denied, and when it has turned into all sorts of malignant and vicious appetites, then we, the middle aged, grow quite distracted and resort to all sorts of restrictive measures. We even try to dam up the sweet fountain itself because we are affrighted by these neglected streams; but almost worse than the restrictive measures is our apparent belief that the city itself has no obligation in the matter, an assumption upon which the modern city turns over to commercialism practically all the provisions for public recreation.

Quite as one set of men has organized the young people into industrial enterprises in order to profit from their toil, so another set of men and also of women, I am sorry to say, have entered the neglected field of recreation and have organized enterprises which make profit out of this invincible love of pleasure.

In every city arise so-called "places"—

"gin-palaces," they are called in fiction; in Chicago we euphemistically say merely "places,"—in which alcohol is dispensed, not to allay thirst, but, ostensibly to stimulate gaiety, it is sold really in order to empty pockets. Huge dance halls are opened to which hundreds of young people are attracted, many of whom stand wistfully outside a roped circle, for it requires five cents to procure within it for five minutes the sense of allurement and intoxication which is sold in lieu of innocent pleasure. These coarse and illicit merrymakings remind one of the unrestrained jollities of Restoration London, and they are indeed their direct descendants, properly commercialized, still confusing joy with lust, and gaiety with debauchery. Since the soldiers of Cromwell shut up the people's playhouses and destroyed their pleasure fields, the Anglo-Saxon city has turned over the provision for public recreation to the most evil-minded and the most unscrupulous members of the community. We see thousands of girls walking up and down the streets on a pleasant evening with no chance to catch a sight of pleasure even through a lighted window, save as these lurid places provide it. Apparently the modern city sees in these girls only two possibilities, both of them commercial: first, a chance to utilize by day their new and tender labor power in its factories and shops, and then another chance in the evening to extract from them their petty wages by pandering to their love of pleasure.

As these overworked girls stream along the street, the rest of us see only the self-conscious walk, the giggling speech, the preposterous clothing. And yet through the huge hat, with its wilderness of bedraggled feathers, the girl announces to the world that she is here. She demands attention to the fact of her existence, she states that she is ready to live, to take her place in the world. The most precious moment in human development is the young creature's assertion that he is unlike any other human being, and has an individual contribution to make to the world. The variation from the established type is at the root of all change, the only possible basis for progress, all that keeps life from growing unprofitably stale and repetitious.

Is it only the artists who really see these young creatures as they are—the artists who are themselves endowed with immortal youth? Is it our disregard of the artist's message which makes us so blind and so stupid, or are we so under the influence of our *Zeitgeist* that we can detect only commercial values in the young as well as in the old? It is as if our eyes were holden to the mystic beauty, the redemptive joy, the civic pride which these multitudes of young people might supply to our dingy towns.

The young creatures themselves piteously look all about them in order to find an adequate means of expression for their most precious message: One day a serious young man came to Hull-House with his pretty young sister who, he explained, wanted to go somewhere every single evening, "although she could only give the flimsy excuse that the flat was too little and too stuffy to stay in." In the difficult rôle of elder brother, he had done his best, stating that he had taken her "to all the

missions in the neighborhood, that she had had
a chance to listen to some awful good sermons
and to some elegant hymns, but that some way
she did not seem to care for the society of the
best Christian people." The little sister
reddened painfully under this cruel indictment
and could offer no word of excuse, but a curious thing happened to me. Perhaps it was the
phrase "the best Christian people," perhaps it
was the delicate color of her flushing cheeks
and her swimming eyes, but certain it is, that
instantly and vividly there appeared to my
mind the delicately tinted piece of wall in a
Roman catacomb where the early Christians,
through a dozen devices of spring flowers,
skipping lambs and a shepherd tenderly guid-
ing the young, had indelibly written down that
the Christian message is one of inexpressible
joy. Who is responsible for forgetting this
message delivered by the "best Christian people" two thousand years ago? Who is to blame
that the lambs, the little ewe lambs, have been
so caught upon the brambles?

But quite as the modern city wastes this
most valuable moment in the life of the girl,

and drives into all sorts of absurd and obscure
expressions her love and yearning towards the
world in which she forecasts her destiny, so it
often drives the boy into gambling and drinking in order to find his adventure.

Of Lincoln's enlistment of two and a half
million soldiers, a very large number were under
twenty-one, some of them under eighteen, and
still others were mere children under fifteen.
Even in those stirring times when patriotism
and high resolve were at the flood, no one re-
sponded as did "the boys," and the great soul
who yearned over them, who refused to shoot the
sentinels who slept the sleep of childhood, knew,
as no one else knew, the precious glowing stuff
of which his army was made. But what of the
millions of boys who are now searching for adventurous action, longing to fulfil the same high
purpose?

One of the most pathetic sights in the public
dance halls of Chicago is the number of young
men, obviously honest young fellows from the
country, who stand about vainly hoping to
make the acquaintance of some "nice girl."
They look eagerly up and down the rows of

girls, many of whom are drawn to the hall by
the same keen desire for pleasure and social
intercourse which the lonely young men themselves feel.

One Sunday night at twelve o'clock I had
occasion to go into a large public dance hall.
As I was standing by the rail looking for the
girl I had come to find, a young man ap-
proached me and quite simply asked me to in-
troduce him to some "nice girl," saying that
he did not know any one there. On my replying
that a public dance hall was not the best place
in which to look for a nice girl, he said: "But
I don't know any other place where there is
a chance to meet any kind of a girl. I'm
awfully lonesome since I came to Chicago."
And then he added rather defiantly: "Some
nice girls do come here! It's one of the best
halls in town." He was voicing the "bitter
loneliness" that many city men remember to
have experienced during the first years after
they had "come up to town." Occasionally
the right sort of man and girl meet each other
in these dance halls and the romance with such
a tawdry beginning ends happily and respect-

ably. But, unfortunately, mingled with the respectable young men seeking to form the acquaintance of young women through the only channel which is available to them, are many young fellows of evil purpose, and among the girls who have left their lonely boarding houses or rigid homes for a "little fling" are likewise women who openly desire to make money from the young men whom they meet, and back of it all is the desire to profit by the sale of intoxicating and "doctored" drinks.

Perhaps never before have the pleasures of the young and mature become so definitely separated as in the modern city. The public dance halls filled with frivolous and irresponsible young people in a feverish search for pleasure, are but a sorry substitute for the old dances on the village green in which all of the older people of the village participated. Chaperonage was not then a social duty but natural and inevitable, and the whole courtship period was guarded by the conventions and restraint which were taken as a matter of course and had developed through years of publicity and simple propriety.

The only marvel is that the stupid attempt to put the fine old wine of traditional country life into the new bottles of the modern town does not lead to disaster oftener than it does, and that the wine so long remains pure and sparkling.

We cannot afford to be ungenerous to the city in which we live without suffering the penalty which lack of fair interpretation always entails. Let us know the modern city in its weakness and wickedness, and then seek to rectify and purify it until it shall be free at least from the grosser temptations which now beset the young people who are living in its tenement houses and working in its factories. The mass of these young people are possessed of good intentions and they are equipped with a certain understanding of city life. This itself could be made a most valuable social instrument toward securing innocent recreation and better social organization. They are already serving the city in so far as it is honeycombed with mutual benefit societies, with "pleasure clubs," with organizations connected with churches and factories which are filling a genuine social need. And yet the whole apparatus for supplying pleasure is wretchedly inadequate and full of danger to whomsoever may approach it. Who is responsible for its inadequacy and dangers? We certainly cannot expect the fathers and mothers who have come to the city from farms or who have emigrated from other lands to appreciate or rectify these dangers. We cannot expect the young people themselves to cling to conventions which are totally unsuited to modern city conditions, nor yet to be equal to the task of forming new conventions through which this more agglomerate social life may express itself. Above all we cannot hope that they will understand the emotional force which seizes them and which, when it does not find the traditional line of domesticity, serves as a cancer in the very tissues of society and as a disrupter of the securest social bonds. No attempt is made to treat the manifestations of this fundamental instinct with dignity or to give it possible social utility. The spontaneous joy, the clamor for pleasure, the desire of the young people to appear finer and better and altogether more lovely than they really are, the idealization not only of each other but of the whole earth which they regard but as a theater for their noble exploits, the unworldly ambitions, the romantic hopes, the make-believe world in which they live, if properly utilized, what might they not do to make our sordid cities more beautiful, more companionable? And yet at the present moment every city is full of young people who are utterly bewildered and uninstructed in regard to the basic experience which must inevitably come to them, and which has varied, remote, and indirect expressions.

Even those who may not agree with the authorities who claim that it is this fundamental sex susceptibility which suffuses the world with its deepest meaning and beauty, and furnishes the momentum towards all art, will perhaps permit me to quote the classical expression of this view as set forth in that ancient and wonderful conversation between Socrates and the wise woman Diotima. Socrates asks: ''What are they doing who show all this eagerness and heat which is called love? And what is the object they have in view?

Answer me." Diotima replies: "I will teach you. The object which they have in view is birth in beauty, whether of body or soul. . . . For love, Socrates, is not as you imagine the love of the beautiful only . . . . but the love of birth in beauty, because to the mortal creature generation is a sort of eternity and immortality."

To emphasize the eternal aspects of love is not of course an easy undertaking, even if we follow the clue afforded by the heart of every generous lover. His experience at least in certain moments tends to pull him on and out from the passion for one to an enthusiasm for that highest beauty and excellence of which the most perfect form is but an inadequate expression. Even the most loutish tenement-house youth vaguely feels this, and at least at rare intervals reveals it in his talk to his "girl." His memory unexpectedly brings hidden treasures to the surface of consciousness and he recalls the more delicate and tender experiences of his childhood and earlier youth. "I remember the time when my little sister died, that I rode out to the cemetery feeling that everybody in Chicago had moved away from the town to make room for that kid's funeral, everything was so darned lonesome and yet it was kind of peaceful too." Or, "I never had a chance to go into the country when I was a kid, but I remember one day when I had to deliver a package way out on the West Side, that I saw a flock of sheep in Douglas Park. I had never thought that a sheep could be anywhere but in a picture, and when I saw those big white spots on the green grass beginning to move and to turn into sheep, I felt exactly as if Saint Cecilia had come out of her frame over the organ and was walking in the park." Such moments come into the life of the most prosaic youth living in the most crowded quarters of the cities. What do we do to encourage and to solidify those moments, to make them come true in our dingy towns, to give them expression in forms of art?

We not only fail in this undertaking but even debase existing forms of art. We are informed by high authority that there is nothing in the environment to which youth so keenly responds as to music, and yet the streets, the vaudeville shows, the five-cent theaters are full of the most blatant and vulgar songs. The trivial and obscene words, the meaningless and flippant airs run through the heads of hundreds of young people for hours at a time while they are engaged in monotonous factory work. We totally ignore that ancient connection between music and morals which was so long insisted upon by philosophers as well as poets. The street music has quite broken away from all control, both of the educator and the patriot, and we have grown singularly careless in regard to its influence upon young people. Although we legislate against it in saloons because of its dangerous influence there, we constantly permit music on the street to incite that which should be controlled, to degrade that which should be exalted, to make sensuous that which might be lifted into the realm of the higher imagination.

Our attitude towards music is typical of our carelessness towards all those things which make for common joy and for the restraints of higher civilization on the streets. It is as if our cities had not yet developed a sense of responsibility in regard to the life of the streets, and continually forget that recreation is stronger than vice, and that recreation alone can stifle the lust for vice.

Perhaps we need to take a page from the philosophy of the Greeks to whom the world of fact was also the world of the ideal, and to whom the realization of what ought to be, involved not the destruction of what was, but merely its perfecting upon its own lines. To the Greeks virtue was not a hard conformity to a law felt as alien to the natural character, but a free expression of the inner life. To treat thus the fundamental susceptibility of sex which now so bewilders the street life and drives young people themselves into all sorts of difficulties, would mean to loosen it from the things of sense and to link it to the affairs of the imagination. It would mean to fit to this gross and heavy stuff the wings of the mind, to scatter from it "the clinging mud of banality and vulgarity," and to speed it on through our city streets amid spontaneous laughter, snatches of lyric song, the recovered forms of old dances, and the traditional rondels of merry games. It would thus bring charm and beauty to the prosaic city and connect it subtly with the arts of the past as well as with the vigor and renewed life of the future.

CHAPTER II

THE WRECKED FOUNDATIONS
OF DOMESTICITY

CHAPTER II

THE WRECKED FOUNDATIONS OF DOMESTICITY

"Sense with keenest edge unused
Yet unsteel'd by scathing fire:
Lovely feet as yet unbruised
On the ways of dark desire!"

These words written by a poet to his young
son express the longing which has at times
seized all of us, to guard youth from the mass
of difficulties which may be traced to the obscure manifestation of that fundamental susceptibility of which we are all slow to speak
and concerning which we evade public responsibility, although it brings its scores of victims
into the police courts every morning.

At the very outset we must bear in mind that
the senses of youth are singularly acute, and
ready to respond to every vivid appeal. We
know that nature herself has sharpened the
senses for her own purposes, and is deliber-

ately establishing a connection between them and the newly awakened susceptibility of sex; for it is only through the outward senses that the selection of an individual mate is made and the instinct utilized for nature's purposes. It would seem, however, that nature was determined that the force and constancy of the instinct must make up for its lack of precision, and that she was totally unconcerned that this instinct ruthlessly seized the youth at the moment when he was least prepared to cope with it; not only because his powers of self-control and discrimination are unequal to the task, but because his senses are helplessly wide open to the world. These early manifestations of the sex susceptibility are for the most part vague and formless, and are absolutely without definition to the youth himself. Sometimes months and years elapse before the individual mate is selected and determined upon, and during the time when the differentiation is not complete— and it often is not—there is of necessity a great deal of groping and waste.

This period of groping is complicated by the fact that the youth's power for appreciating is far ahead of his ability for expression. "The inner traffic fairly obstructs the outer current," and it is nothing short of cruelty to over-stimulate his senses as does the modern city. This period is difficult everywhere, but it seems at times as if a great city almost deliberately increased its perils. The newly awakened senses are appealed to by all that is gaudy and sensual, by the flippant street music, the highly colored theater posters, the trashy love stories, the feathered hats, the cheap heroics of the revolvers displayed in the pawn-shop windows. This fundamental susceptibility is thus evoked without a corresponding stir of the higher imagination, and the result is as dangerous as possible. We are told upon good authority that "If the imagination is retarded, while the senses remain awake, we have a state of esthetic insensibility,"—in other words, the senses become sodden and cannot be lifted from the ground. It is this state of "esthetic insensibility" into which we allow the youth to fall which is so distressing and so unjustifiable. Sex impulse then becomes merely a dumb and powerful instinct without in the least awakening the imagination or the heart, nor does it overflow into neighboring fields of consciousness. Every city contains hundreds of degenerates who have been over-mastered and borne down by it; they fill the casual lodging houses and the infirmaries. In many instances it has pushed men of ability and promise to the bottom of the social scale. Warner, in his *American Charities*, designates it as one of the steady forces making for failure and poverty, and contends that "the inherent uncleanness of their minds prevents many men from rising above the rank of day laborers and finally incapacitates them even for that position." He also suggests that the modern man has a stronger imagination than the man of a few hundred years ago and that sensuality destroys him the more rapidly.

It is difficult to state how much evil and distress might be averted if the imagination were utilized in its higher capacities through the historic paths. An English moralist has lately asserted that "much of the evil of the time may be traced to outraged imagination. It is the strongest quality of the brain and it is starved.

Children, from their earliest years, are hedged
in with facts; they are not trained to use their
minds on the unseen.''

In failing to diffuse and utilize this fundamental instinct of sex through the imagination,
we not only inadvertently foster vice and en-
ervation, but we throw away one of the most
precious implements for ministering to life's
highest needs. There is no doubt that this ill
adjusted function consumes quite unnecessa-
rily vast stores of vital energy, even when
we contemplate it in its immature manifestations which are infinitely more wholesome
than the dumb swamping process. Every high
school boy and girl knows the difference between the concentration and the diffusion of
this impulse, although they would be hopelessly bewildered by the use of the terms.
They will declare one of their companions to
be "in love" if his fancy is occupied by the
image of a single person about whom all the
newly found values gather, and without whom
his solitude is an eternal melancholy. But if
the stimulus does not appear as a definite
image, and the values evoked are dispensed

over the world, the young person suddenly
seems to have discovered a beauty and significance in many things—he responds to poetry,
he becomes a lover of nature, he is filled with
religious devotion or with philanthropic zeal.
Experience, with young people, easily illus-
trates the possibility and value of diffusion.

It is neither a short nor an easy undertaking
to substitute the love of beauty for mere desire, to place the mind above the senses; but
is not this the sum of the immemorial obligation which rests upon the adults of each
generation if they would nurture and restrain
the youth, and has not the whole history of
civilization been but one long effort to substitute psychic impulsion for the driving force
of blind appetite?

Society has recognized the "imitative play"
impulse of children and provides them with
tiny bricks with which to "build a house," and
dolls upon which they may lavish their tenderness. We exalt the love of the mother and the
stability of the home, but in regard to those
difficult years between childhood and maturity
we beg the question and unless we repress, we

do nothing. We are so timid and inconsistent that although we declare the home to be the foundation of society, we do nothing to direct the force upon which the continuity of the home depends. And yet to one who has lived for years in a crowded quarter where men, women and children constantly jostle each other and press upon every inch of space in shop, tenement and street, nothing is more impressive than the strength, the continuity, the varied and powerful manifestations, of family affection. It goes without saying that every tenement house contains women who for years spend their hurried days in preparing food and clothing and pass their sleepless nights in tending and nursing their exigent children, with never one thought for their own comfort or pleasure or development save as these may be connected with the future of their families. We all know as a matter of course that every shop is crowded with workingmen who year after year spend all of their wages upon the nurture and education of their children, reserving for themselves but the shabbiest clothing and a crowded place at the family table.

"Bad weather for you to be out in," you remark on a February evening, as you meet rheumatic Mr. S. hobbling home through the freezing sleet without an overcoat. "Yes, it is bad," he assents: "but I've walked to work all this last year. We've sent the oldest boy back to high school, you know," and he moves on with no thought that he is doing other than fulfilling the ordinary lot of the ordinary man.

These are the familiar and the constant manifestations of family affection which are so intimate a part of life that we scarcely observe them.

In addition to these we find peculiar manifestations of family devotion exemplifying that touching affection which rises to unusual sacrifice because it is close to pity and feebleness. "My cousin and his family had to go back to Italy. He got to Ellis Island with his wife and five children, but they wouldn't let in the feeble-minded boy, so of course they all went back with him. My cousin was fearful disappointed.''

Or, ''These are the five children of my brother. He and his wife, my father and mother, were all done for in the bad time at Kishinef. It's up to me all right to take care of the kids, and I'd no more go back on them than I would on my own.'' Or, again: ''Yes, I have seven children of my own. My husband died when Tim was born. The other three children belong to my sister, who died the year after my husband. I get on pretty well. I scrub in a factory every night from six to twelve, and I go out washing four days a week. So far the children have all gone through the eighth grade before they quit school,'' she concludes, beaming with pride and joy.

That wonderful devotion to the child seems at times, in the midst of our stupid social and industrial arrangements, all that keeps society human, the touch of nature which unites it, as it was that same devotion which first lifted it out of the swamp of bestiality. The devotion to the child is ''the inevitable conclusion of the two premises of the practical syllogism, the devotion of man to woman.'' It is, of course, this tremendous force which makes possible the family, that bond which holds society together and blends the experience of generations into a continuous story. The family has been called ''the fountain of morality,'' ''the source of law,'' ''the necessary prelude to the state'' itself; but while it is continuous historically, this dual bond must be made anew a myriad times in each generation, and the forces upon which its formation depend must be powerful and unerring. It would be too great a risk to leave it to a force whose manifestations are intermittent and uncertain. The desired result is too grave and fundamental.

One Sunday evening an excited young man came to see me, saying that he must have advice; some one must tell him at once what to do, as his wife was in the state's prison serving a sentence for a crime which he himself had committed. He had seen her the day before, and though she had been there only a month he was convinced that she was developing consumption. She was ''only seventeen,

and couldn't stand the hard work and the
'low down' women'' whom she had for companions. My remark that a girl of seventeen
was too young to be in the state penitentiary
brought out the whole wretched story.

He had been unsteady for many years and
the despair of his thoroughly respectable family who had sent him West the year before.
In Arkansas he had fallen in love with a girl of
sixteen and married her. His mother was far
from pleased, but had finally sent him money
to bring his bride to Chicago, in the hope that
he might settle there. *En route* they stopped
at a small town for the naïve reason that he
wanted to have an aching tooth pulled. But
the tooth gave him an excellent opportunity
to have a drink, and before he reached the
office of the country practitioner he was in-
toxicated. As they passed through the vesti-
bule he stole an overcoat hanging there,
although the little wife piteously begged him
to let it alone. Out of sheer bravado he
carried it across his arm as they walked down
the street, and was, of course, immediately
arrested ''with the goods upon him.'' In sheer

terror of being separated from her husband, the wife insisted that she had been an accomplice, and together they were put into the county jail awaiting the action of the Grand Jury. At the end of the sixth week, on one of the rare occasions when they were permitted to talk to each other through the grating which separated the men's visiting quarters from the women's, the young wife told her husband that she made up her mind to swear that she had stolen the overcoat. What could she do if he were sent to prison and she were left free? She was afraid to go to his people and could not possibly go back to hers. In spite of his protest, that very night she sent for the state's attorney and made a full confession, giving her age as eighteen in the hope of making her testimony more valuable. From that time on they stuck to the lie through the indictment, the trial and her conviction. Apparently it had seemed to him only a well-arranged plot until he had visited the penitentiary the day before, and had really seen her piteous plight. Remorse had seized him at last, and he was ready to make every restitution. She, however, had no notion of giving up—on the contrary, as she realized more clearly what prison life meant, she was daily more determined to spare him the experience. Her letters, written in the unformed hand of a child—for her husband had himself taught her to read and write—were filled with a riot of self-abnegation, the martyr's joy as he feels the iron enter the flesh. Thus had an illiterate, neglected girl through sheer devotion to a worthless sort of young fellow inclined to drink, entered into that noble company of martyrs.

When girls "go wrong" what happens? How has this tremendous force, valuable and necessary for the foundation of the family, become misdirected? When its manifestations follow the legitimate channels of wedded life we call them praiseworthy; but there are other manifestations quite outside the legal and moral channels which yet compel our admiration.

A young woman of my acquaintance was married to a professional criminal named Joe. Three months after the wedding he was ar-

rested and "sent up" for two years. Molly
had always been accustomed to many lovers,
but she remained faithful to her absent husband for a year. At the end of that time she
obtained a divorce which the state law makes
easy for the wife of a convict, and married a
man who was "rich and respectable"—in fact,
he owned the small manufacturing establishment in which her mother did the scrubbing.
He moved his bride to another part of town
six miles away, provided her with a "steam-
heated flat," furniture upholstered in "cut
velvet," and many other luxuries of which
Molly heretofore had only dreamed. One day
as she was wheeling a handsome baby carriage
up and down the prosperous street, her
brother, who was "Joe's pal," came to tell
her that Joe was "out," had come to the old
tenement and was "mighty sore" because "she
had gone back on him." Without a moment's
hesitation Molly turned the baby carriage in
the direction of her old home and never stopped
wheeling it until she had compassed the entire
six miles. She and Joe rented the old room
and went to housekeeping. The rich and re-

spectable husband made every effort to persuade her to come back, and then another series of efforts to recover his child, before he set her free through a court proceeding. Joe, however, steadfastly refused to marry her, still "sore" because she had not "stood by." As he worked only intermittently, and was too closely supervised by the police to do much at his old occupation, Molly was obliged to support the humble ménage by scrubbing in a neighboring lodging house and by washing "the odd shirts" of the lodgers. For five years, during which time two children were born, when she was constantly subjected to the taunts of her neighbors, and when all the charitable agencies refused to give help to such an irregular household, Molly happily went on her course with no shade of regret or sorrow. "I'm all right as long as Joe keeps out of the jug," was her slogan of happiness, low in tone, perhaps, but genuine and "game." Her surroundings were as sordid as possible, consisting of a constantly changing series of cheap "furnished rooms" in which the battered baby carriage was the sole witness of better days. But Molly's heart was full of courage and happiness, and she was never desolate until her criminal lover was "sent up" again, this time on a really serious charge.

These irregular manifestations form a link between that world in which each one struggles to "live respectable," and that nether world in which are also found cases of devotion and of enduring affection arising out of the midst of the folly and the shame. The girl there who through all tribulation supports her recreant "lover," or the girl who overcomes her drink and opium habits, who renounces luxuries and goes back to uninteresting daily toil for the sake of the good opinion of a man who wishes her to "appear decent," although he never means to marry her, these are also impressive.

One of our earliest experiences at Hull-House had to do with a lover of this type and the charming young girl who had become fatally attached to him. I can see her now running for protection up the broad steps of the columned piazza then surrounding Hull-House. Her slender figure was trembling with fright, her tear-covered face swollen and bloodstained from the blows he had dealt her. "He is apt to abuse me when he is drunk," was the only explanation, and that given by way of apology, which could be extracted from her. When we discovered that there had been no marriage ceremony, that there were no living children, that she had twice narrowly escaped losing her life, it seemed a simple matter to insist that the relation should be broken off. She apathetically remained at Hull-House for a few weeks, but when her strength had somewhat returned, when her lover began to recover from his prolonged debauch of whiskey and opium, she insisted upon going home every day to prepare his meals and to see that the little tenement was clean and comfortable because "Pierre is always so sick and weak after one of those long ones." This of course meant that she was drifting back to him, and when she was at last restrained by that moral compulsion, by that overwhelming of another's will which is always so ruthlessly exerted by those who are conscious that virtue is struggling with vice, her mind gave way and she became utterly distraught.

A poor little Ophelia, I met her one night wandering in the hall half dressed in the tawdry pink gown "that Pierre liked best of all" and groping on the blank wall to find the door which might permit her to escape to her lover. In a few days it was obvious that hospital restraint was necessary, but when she finally recovered we were obliged to admit that there is no civic authority which can control the acts of a girl of eighteen. From the hospital she followed her heart directly back to Pierre, who had in the meantime moved out of the Hull-House neighborhood. We knew later that he had degraded the poor child still further by obliging her to earn money for his drugs by that last method resorted to by a degenerate man to whom a woman's devotion still clings.

It is inevitable that a force which is enduring enough to withstand the discouragements, the suffering and privation of daily living, strenuous enough to overcome and rectify the impulses which make for greed and self-indulgence, should be able, even under untoward

conditions, to lift up and transfigure those who
are really within its grasp and set them in
marked contrast to those who are merely playing a game with it or using it for gain. But
what has happened to these wretched girls?
Why has this beneficent current cast them
upon the shores of death and destruction when
it should have carried them into the safe port
of domesticity? Through whose fault has this
basic emotion served merely to trick and de-
ride them?

Older nations have taken a well defined line
of action in regard to it.

Among the Hull-House neighbors are many
of the Latin races who employ a careful chaperonage over their marriageable daughters and
provide husbands for them at an early age.
"My father will get a husband for me this
winter," announces Angelina, whose father has
brought her to a party at Hull-House, and she
adds with a toss of her head, "I saw two already, but my father says they haven't
saved enough money to marry me." She
feels quite as content in her father's wis-
dom and ability to provide her with a

husband as she does in his capacity to escort her home safely from the party. He does not permit her to cross the threshold after nightfall unaccompanied by himself, and unless the dowry and the husband are provided before she is eighteen he will consider himself derelict in his duty towards her. "Francesca can't even come to the Sodality meeting this winter. She lives only across from the church but her mother won't let her come because her father is out West working on a railroad," is a comment one often hears. The system works well only when it is carried logically through to the end of an early marriage with a properly-provided husband.

Even with the Latin races, when the system is tried in America it often breaks down, and when the Anglo-Saxons anywhere imitate this régime it is usually utterly futile. They follow the first part of the program as far as repression is concerned, but they find it impossible to follow the second because all sorts of inherited notions deter them. The repressed girl, if she is not one of the languishing type, takes matters into her own hands, and finds her pleasures in illicit ways, without her parents' knowledge. "I had no idea my daughter was going to public dances. She always told me she was spending the night with her cousin on the South Side. I hadn't a suspicion of the truth," many a broken-hearted mother explains. An officer who has had a long experience in the Juvenile Court of Chicago, and has listened to hundreds of cases involving wayward girls, gives it as his deliberate impression that a large majority of cases are from families where the discipline had been rigid, where they had taken but half of the convention of the Old World and left the other half.

Unless we mean to go back to these Old World customs which are already hopelessly broken, there would seem to be but one path open to us in America. That path implies freedom for the young people made safe only through their own self-control. This, in turn, must be based upon knowledge and habits of clean companionship. In point of fact no course between the two is safe in a modern city, and in the most crowded quarters the young people themselves are working out a

protective code which reminds one of the in-
stinctive protection that the free-ranging child
in the country learns in regard to poisonous
plants and "marshy places," or of the cautions
and abilities that the mountain child develops
in regard to ice and precipices. This statement, of course, does not hold good concerning a large number of children in every crowded
city quarter who may be classed as degenerates, the children of careless or dissolute
mothers who fall into all sorts of degenerate
habits and associations before childhood is
passed, who cannot be said to have "gone
wrong" at any one moment because they have
never been in the right path even of innocent
childhood; but the statement is sound concerning thousands of girls who go to and from
work every day with crowds of young men
who meet them again and again in the occasional evening pleasures of the more decent
dance halls or on a Sunday afternoon in the
parks.

The mothers who are of most use to these
normal city working girls are the mothers who
develop a sense of companionship with the

changing experiences of their daughters, who are willing to modify ill-fitting social conventions into rules of conduct which are of actual service to their children in their daily lives of factory work and of city amusements. Those mothers, through their sympathy and adaptability, substitute keen present interests and activity for solemn warnings and restraint, self-expression for repression. Their vigorous family life allies itself by a dozen bonds to the educational, the industrial and the recreational organizations of the modern city, and makes for intelligent understanding, industrial efficiency and sane social pleasures.

By all means let us preserve the safety of the home, but let us also make safe the street in which the majority of our young people find their recreation and form their permanent relationships. Let us not forget that the great processes of social life develop themselves through influences of which each participant is unconscious as he struggles alone and unaided in the strength of a current which seizes him and bears him along with myriads of others, a current which may so easily wreck the very foundations of domesticity.

CHAPTER III
THE QUEST FOR ADVENTURE

CHAPTER III

THE QUEST FOR ADVENTURE

A certain number of the outrages upon the spirit of youth may be traced to degenerate or careless parents who totally neglect their responsibilities; a certain other large number of wrongs are due to sordid men and women who deliberately use the legitimate pleasure-seeking of young people as lures into vice. There remains, however, a third very large class of offenses for which the community as a whole must be held responsible if it would escape the condemnation, "Woe unto him by whom offenses come." This class of offenses is traceable to a dense ignorance on the part of the average citizen as to the requirements of youth, and to a persistent blindness on the part of educators as to youth's most obvious needs.

The young people are overborne by their own undirected and misguided energies. A mere temperamental outbreak in a brief period of obstreperousness exposes a promising boy to arrest and imprisonment, an accidental combination of circumstances too complicated and overwhelming to be coped with by an immature mind, condemns a growing lad to a criminal career. These impulsive misdeeds may be thought of as dividing into two great trends somewhat obscurely analogous to the two historic divisions of man's motive power, for we are told that all the activities of primitive man and even those of his more civilized successors may be broadly traced to the impulsion of two elemental appetites. The first drove him to the search for food, the hunt developing into war with neighboring tribes and finally broadening into barter and modern commerce; the second urged him to secure and protect a mate, developing into domestic life, widening into the building of homes and cities, into the cultivation of the arts and a care for beauty.

In the life of each boy there comes a time when these primitive instincts urge him to action, when he is himself frightened by their undefined power. He is faced by the necessity of taming them, of reducing them to manageable impulses just at the moment when "a boy's will is the wind's will," or, in the words of a veteran educator, at the time when "it is almost impossible for an adult to realize the boy's irresponsibility and even moral neurasthenia." That the boy often fails may be traced in those pitiful figures which show that between two and three times as much incorrigibility occurs between the ages of thirteen and sixteen as at any other period of life.

The second division of motive power has been treated in the preceding chapter. The present chapter is an effort to point out the necessity for an understanding of the first trend of motives if we would minimize the temptations of the struggle and free the boy from the constant sense of the stupidity and savagery of life. To set his feet in the worn path of civilization is not an easy task, but it may give us a clue for the undertaking to trace his misdeeds to the unrecognized and primitive spirit of adventure corresponding to the old activity of the hunt, of warfare, and of discovery.

To do this intelligently, we shall have to
remember that many boys in the years
immediately following school find no restraint
either in tradition or character. They drop
learning as a childish thing and look upon
school as a tiresome task that is finished. They
demand pleasure as the right of one who earns
his own living. They have developed no capacity for recreation demanding mental effort or
even muscular skill, and are obliged to seek
only that depending upon sight, sound and
taste. Many of them begin to pay board to
their mothers, and make the best bargain they
can, that more money may be left to spend in
the evening. They even bait the excitement of
"losing a job," and often provoke a foreman
if only to see "how much he will stand."
They are constitutionally unable to enjoy anything continuously and follow their vagrant
wills unhindered. Unfortunately the city
lends itself to this distraction. At the best, it
is difficult to know what to select and what
to eliminate as objects of attention among its
thronged streets, its glittering shops, its gaudy
advertisements of shows and amusements. It

is perhaps to the credit of many city boys that the very first puerile spirit of adventure looking abroad in the world for material upon which to exercise itself, seems to center about the railroad. The impulse is not unlike that which excites the coast-dwelling lad to dream of

> "The beauty and mystery of the ships
> And the magic of the sea."

I cite here a dozen charges upon which boys were brought into the Juvenile Court of Chicago, all of which might be designated as deeds of adventure. A surprising number, as the reader will observe, are connected with railroads. They are taken from the court records and repeat the actual words used by police officers, irate neighbors, or discouraged parents, when the boys were brought before the judge. (1) Building fires along the railroad tracks; (2) flagging trains; (3) throwing stones at moving train windows; (4) shooting at the actors in the Olympic Theatre with sling shots; (5) breaking signal lights on the railroad; (6) stealing linseed oil barrels from the railroad to make a fire; (7) taking waste from an axle

box and burning it upon the railroad tracks;
(8) turning a switch and running a street car
off the track; (9) staying away from home to
sleep in barns; (10) setting fire to a barn in
order to see the fire engines come up the street;
(11) knocking down signs; (12) cutting West-
ern Union cable.

Another dozen charges also taken from actual
court records might be added as illustrating
the spirit of adventure, for although stealing
is involved in all of them, the deeds were doubtless inspired much more by the adventurous
impulse than by a desire for the loot itself:
(1) Stealing thirteen pigeons from a barn;
(2) stealing a bathing suit; (3) stealing a tent;
(4) stealing ten dollars from mother with which
to buy a revolver; (5) stealing a horse blanket
to use at night when it was cold sleeping
on the wharf; (6) breaking a seal on a freight
car to steal ''grain for chickens''; (7) stealing
apples from a freight car; (8) stealing a candy
peddler's wagon ''to be full up just for once'';
(9) stealing a hand car; (10) stealing a bicycle
to take a ride; (11) stealing a horse and buggy
and driving twenty-five miles into the country;

(12) stealing a stray horse on the prairie and trying to sell it for twenty dollars.

Of another dozen it might be claimed that they were also due to this same adventurous spirit, although the first six were classed as disorderly conduct: (1) Calling a neighbor a "scab"; (2) breaking down a fence; (3) flipping cars; (4) picking up coal from railroad tracks; (5) carrying a concealed "dagger," and stabbing a playmate with it; (6) throwing stones at a railroad employee. The next three were called vagrancy: (1) Loafing on the docks; (2) "sleeping out" nights; (3) getting "wandering spells." One, designated petty larceny, was cutting telephone wires under the sidewalk and selling them; another, called burglary, was taking locks off from basement doors; and the last one bore the dignified title of "resisting an officer" because the boy, who was riding on the fender of a street car, refused to move when an officer ordered him off.

Of course one easily recalls other cases in which the manifestations were negative. I remember an exasperated and frightened mother who took a boy of fourteen into court upon the charge of incorrigibility. She accused him of "shooting craps," "smoking cigarettes," "keeping bad company," "being idle." The mother regrets it now, however, for she thinks that taking a boy into court only gives him a bad name, and that "the police are down on a boy who has once been in court, and that that makes it harder for him." She hardly recognizes her once troublesome charge in the steady young man of nineteen who brings home all his wages and is the pride and stay of her old age.

I recall another boy who worked his way to New York and back again to Chicago before he was quite fourteen years old, skilfully escaping the truant officers as well as the police and special railroad detectives. He told his story with great pride, but always modestly admitted that he could never have done it if his father had not been a locomotive engineer so that he had played around railroad tracks and "was onto them ever since he was a small kid."

There are many of these adventurous boys who exhibit a curious incapacity for any effort which requires sustained energy. They show an absolute lack of interest in the accomplishment of what they undertake, so marked that if challenged in the midst of their activity, they will be quite unable to tell you the end they have in view. Then there are those tramp boys who are the despair of every one who tries to deal with them.

I remember the case of a boy who traveled almost around the world in the years lying between the ages of eleven and fifteen. He had lived for six months in Honolulu where he had made up his mind to settle when the irresistible "Wanderlust" again seized him. He was scrupulously neat in his habits and something of a dandy in appearance. He boasted that he had never stolen, although he had been arrested several times on the charge of vagrancy, a fate which befell him in Chicago and landed him in the Detention Home connected with the Juvenile Court. The judge gained a personal hold upon him, and the lad tried with all the powers of his untrained moral nature to "make good and please the judge." Monotonous factory work was not to be thought of in connection with him, but his good friend the judge found a place for him as a bell-boy in a men's club, where it was hoped that the uniform and the variety of experience might enable him to take the first steps toward regular pay and a settled life. Through another bell-boy, however, he heard of the find of a diamond carelessly left in one of the wash rooms of the club. The chance to throw out mysterious hints of its whereabouts, to bargain for its restoration, to tell of great diamond deals he had heard of in his travels, inevitably laid him open to suspicion which resulted in his dismissal, although he had had nothing to do with the matter beyond gloating over its adventurous aspects. In spite of skilful efforts made to detain him, he once more started on his travels, throwing out such diverse hints as that of "a trip into Old Mexico," or "following up Roosevelt into Africa."

There is an entire series of difficulties directly traceable to the foolish and adventurous persistence of carrying loaded firearms. The morning paper of the day in which I am writing records the following:

"A party of boys, led by Daniel O'Brien, thirteen years old, had gathered in front of the house and O'Brien was throwing stones at Nieczgodzki in revenge for a whipping that he received at his hands about a month ago. The Polish boy ordered them away and threatened to go into the house and get a revolver if they did not stop. Pfister, one of the boys in O'Brien's party, called him a coward, and when he pulled a revolver from his pocket, dared him to put it away and meet him in a fist fight in the street. Instead of accepting the challenge, Nieczgodzki aimed his revolver at Pfister and fired. The bullet crashed through the top of his head and entered the brain. He was rushed to the Alexian Brothers' Hospital, but died a short time after being received there. Nieczgodzki was arrested and held without bail."

This tale could be duplicated almost every morning; what might be merely a boyish scrap is turned into a tragedy because some boy has a revolver.

Many citizens in Chicago have been made heartsick during the past month by the knowledge that a boy of nineteen was lodged in the county jail awaiting the death penalty. He had shot and killed a policeman during the scrimmage of an arrest, although the offense for which he was being "taken in" was a trifling one. His parents came to Chicago twenty years ago from a little farm in Ohio,

the best type of Americans, whom we boast to
be the backbone of our cities. The mother,
who has aged and sickened since the trial,
can only say that "Davie was never a bad boy
until about five years ago when he began to go
with this gang who are always looking out
for fun."

Then there are those piteous cases due to a
perfervid imagination which fails to find material suited to its demands. I can recall mis-
adventures of children living within a few
blocks of Hull-House which may well fill with
chagrin those of us who are trying to admin-
ister to their deeper needs. I remember a
Greek boy of fifteen who was arrested for
attempting to hang a young Turk, stirred by
some vague notion of carrying on a traditional
warfare, and of adding another page to the
heroic annals of Greek history. When sifted,
the incident amounted to little more than a
graphic threat and the lad was dismissed by the
court, covered with confusion and remorse that
he had brought disgrace upon the name of
Greece when he had hoped to add to its glory.

I remember with a lump in my throat the

Bohemian boy of thirteen who committed suicide because he could not "make good" in school, and wished to show that he too had "the stuff" in him, as stated in the piteous little letter left behind. This same love of excitement, the desire to jump out of the humdrum experience of life, also induces boys to experiment with drinks and drugs to a surprising extent. For several years the residents of Hull-House struggled with the difficulty of prohibiting the sale of cocaine to minors under a totally inadequate code of legislation, which has at last happily been changed to one more effective and enforcible. The long effort brought us into contact with dozens of boys who had become victims of the cocaine habit. The first group of these boys was discovered in the house of "Army George." This one-armed man sold cocaine on the streets and also in the levee district by a system of signals so that the word cocaine need never be mentioned, and the style and size of the package was changed so often that even a vigilant police found it hard to locate it. What could be more exciting to a lad than a traffic in a contraband article, carried on in this mysterious fashion? I recall our experience with a gang of boys living on a neighboring street. There were eight of them altogether, the eldest seventeen years of age, the youngest thirteen, and they practically lived the life of vagrants. What answered to their club house was a corner lot on Harrison and Desplaines Streets, strewn with old boilers, in which they slept by night and many times by day. The gang was brought to the attention of Hull-House during the summer of 1904 by a distracted mother, who suspected that they were all addicted to some drug. She was terribly frightened over the state of her youngest boy of thirteen, who was hideously emaciated and his mind reduced almost to vacancy. I remember the poor woman as she sat in the reception room at Hull-House, holding the unconscious boy in her arms, rocking herself back and forth in her fright and despair, saying: "I have seen them go with the drink, and eat the hideous opium, but I never knew anything like this."

An investigation showed that cocaine had first been offered to these boys on the street by a colored man, an agent of a drug store, who had given them samples and urged them to try it. In three or four months they had become hopelessly addicted to its use, and at the end of six months, when they were brought to Hull-House, they were all in a critical condition. At that time not one of them was either going to school or working. They stole from their parents, "swiped junk," pawned their clothes and shoes,—did any desperate thing to "get the dope," as they called it.

Of course they continually required more, and had spent as much as eight dollars a night for cocaine, which they used to "share and share alike." It sounds like a large amount, but it really meant only four doses each during the night, as at that time they were taking twenty-five cents' worth at once if they could possibly secure it. The boys would tell nothing for three or four days after they were discovered, in spite of the united efforts of their families, the police, and the residents of Hull-House. But finally the superior boy of the gang, the manliest and the least debauched, told his tale, and the others followed in quick succession. They were willing to go somewhere to be helped, and were even eager if they could go together, and finally seven of them were sent to the Presbyterian Hospital for four weeks' treatment and afterwards all went to the country together for six weeks more. The emaciated child gained twenty pounds during his sojourn in the hospital, the head of which testified that at least three of the boys could have stood but little more of the irregular living and doping. At the present moment they are all, save one, doing well, although they were rescued so late that they seemed to have but little chance. One is still struggling with the appetite on an Iowa farm and dares not trust himself in the city because he knows too well how cocaine may be procured in spite of better legislation. It is doubtful whether these boys could ever have been pulled through unless they had been allowed to keep together through the hospital and convalescing period,—unless we had been able to utilize the gang spirit and to turn its collective force towards overcoming the desire for the drug.

The desire to dream and see visions also plays an important part with the boys who habitually use cocaine. I recall a small hut used by boys for this purpose. They washed dishes in a neighboring restaurant and as soon as they had earned a few cents they invested in cocaine which they kept pinned underneath their suspenders. When they had accumulated enough for a real debauch they went to this hut and for several days were dead to the outside world. One boy told me that in his dreams he saw large rooms paved with gold and silver money, the walls papered with greenbacks, and that he took away in buckets all that he could carry.

This desire for adventure also seizes girls. A group of girls ranging in age from twelve to seventeen was discovered in Chicago last June, two of whom were being trained by older women to open tills in small shops, to pick pockets, to remove handkerchiefs, furs and purses and to lift merchandise from the counters of department stores. All the articles stolen were at once taken to their teachers and the girls themselves received no remuneration, except

occasional sprees to the theaters or other places
of amusement. The girls gave no coherent
reason for their actions beyond the statement
that they liked the excitement and the fun
of it. Doubtless to the thrill of danger was
added the pleasure and interest of being daily
in the shops and the glitter of "down town."
The boys are more indifferent to this downtown life, and are apt to carry on their adventures on the docks, the railroad tracks or best
of all upon the unoccupied prairie.

This inveterate demand of youth that life
shall afford a large element of excitement is in
a measure well founded. We know of course
that it is necessary to accept excitement as an
inevitable part of recreation, that the first step
in recreation is "that excitement which stirs
the worn or sleeping centers of a man's body
and mind." It is only when it is followed by
nothing else that it defeats its own end, that
it uses up strength and does not create it. In
the actual experience of these boys the excitement has demoralized them and led them into
law-breaking. When, however, they seek legitimate pleasure, and say with great pride that

they are "ready to pay for it," what they find is legal but scarcely more wholesome,—it is still merely excitement. "Looping the loop" amid shrieks of simulated terror or dancing in disorderly saloon halls, are perhaps the natural reactions to a day spent in noisy factories and in trolley cars whirling through the distracting streets, but the city which permits them to be the acme of pleasure and recreation to its young people, commits a grievous mistake.

May we not assume that this love for excitement, this desire for adventure, is basic, and will be evinced by each generation of city boys as a challenge to their elders? And yet those of us who live in Chicago are obliged to confess that last year there were arrested and brought into court fifteen thousand young people under the age of twenty, who had failed to keep even the common law of the land. Most of these young people had broken the law in their blundering efforts to find adventure and in response to the old impulse for self-expression. It is said indeed that practically the whole machinery of the grand jury and of the criminal courts is maintained and operated for the

benefit of youths between the ages of thirteen
and twenty-five. Men up to ninety years of
age, it is true, commit crimes, but they are not
characterized by the recklessness, the bravado
and the horror which have stained our records
in Chicago. An adult with the most sordid
experience of life and the most rudimentary
notion of prudence, could not possibly have
committed them. Only a utilization of that
sudden burst of energy belonging partly to the
future could have achieved them, only a cap-
ture of the imagination and of the deepest emotions of youth could have prevented them!

Possibly these fifteen thousand youths were
brought to grief because the adult population
assumed that the young would be able to grasp
only that which is presented in the form of
sensation; as if they believed that youth could
thus early become absorbed in a hand to mouth
existence, and so entangled in materialism that
there would be no reaction against it. It is as
though we were deaf to the appeal of these
young creatures, claiming their share of the joy
of life, flinging out into the dingy city their
desires and aspirations after unknown realities,

their unutterable longings for companionship and pleasure. Their very demand for excitement is a protest against the dulness of life, to which we ourselves instinctively respond.

CHAPTER IV
THE HOUSE OF DREAMS

CHAPTER IV

THE HOUSE OF DREAMS

To the preoccupied adult who is prone to use the city street as a mere passageway from one hurried duty to another, nothing is more touching than his encounter with a group of children and young people who are emerging from a theater with the magic of the play still thick upon them. They look up and down the familiar street scarcely recognizing it and quite unable to determine the direction of home. From a tangle of "make believe" they gravely scrutinize the real world which they are so reluctant to reënter, reminding one of the absorbed gaze of a child who is groping his way back from fairy-land whither the story has completely transported him.

"Going to the show" for thousands of young people in every industrial city is the only possible road to the realms of mystery and romance; the theater is the only place where they can satisfy that craving for a conception of life higher than that which the actual world offers them. In a very real sense the drama and the drama alone performs for them the office of art as is clearly revealed in their blundering demand stated in many forms for "a play unlike life." The theater becomes to them a "veritable house of dreams" infinitely more real than the noisy streets and the crowded factories.

This first simple demand upon the theater for romance is closely allied to one more complex which might be described as a search for solace and distraction in those moments of first awakening from the glamour of a youth's interpretation of life to the sterner realities which are thrust upon his consciousness. These perceptions which inevitably "close around" and imprison the spirit of youth are perhaps never so grim as in the case of the wage-earning child. We can all recall our own moments of revolt against life's actualities, our reluctance to admit that all life was to be as unheroic and uneventful as that which we saw about us, it was too unbearable that "this was all there was" and we tried every possible avenue of escape. As we made an effort to believe, in spite of what we saw, that life was noble and harmonious, as we stubbornly clung to poesy in contradiction to the testimony of our senses, so we see thousands of young people thronging the theaters bent in their turn upon the same quest. The drama provides a transition between the romantic conceptions which they vainly struggle to keep intact and life's cruelties and trivialities which they refuse to admit. A child whose imagination has been cultivated is able to do this for himself through reading and reverie, but for the overworked city youth of meager education, perhaps nothing but the theater is able to perform this important office.

The theater also has a strange power to forecast life for the youth. Each boy comes from our ancestral past not "in entire forgetfulness," and quite as he unconsciously uses ancient war-cries in his street play, so he longs to reproduce and to see set before him the valors and vengeances of a society embodying a much more primitive state of morality than that in which he finds himself. Mr. Patten has pointed out that the elemental action which the stage presents, the old emotions of love and jealousy, of revenge and daring take the thoughts of the spectator back into deep and well worn channels in which his mind runs with a sense of rest afforded by nothing else. The cheap drama brings cause and effect, will power and action, once more into relation and gives a man the thrilling conviction that he may yet be master of his fate. The youth of course, quite unconscious of this psychology, views the deeds of the hero simply as a forecast of his own future and it is this fascinating view of his own career which draws the boy to "shows" of all sorts. They can scarcely be too improbable for him, portraying, as they do, his belief in his own prowess. A series of slides which has lately been very popular in the five-cent theaters of Chicago, portrayed five masked men breaking into a humble dwelling, killing the father of the family and carrying away the family treasure. The golden-haired son of the house, aged seven, vows eternal vengeance on the spot, and follows one villain after

another to his doom. The execution of each is
shown in lurid detail, and the last slide of the
series depicts the hero, aged ten, kneeling
upon his father's grave counting on the fingers
of one hand the number of men that he has
killed, and thanking God that he has been
permitted to be an instrument of vengeance.

In another series of slides, a poor woman
is wearily bending over some sewing, a baby
is crying in the cradle, and two little boys of
nine and ten are asking for food. In despair
the mother sends them out into the street to
beg, but instead they steal a revolver from a
pawn shop and with it kill a Chinese laundry-
man, robbing him of $200. They rush home
with the treasure which is found by the mother
in the baby's cradle, whereupon she and her sons
fall upon their knees and send up a prayer of
thankfulness for this timely and heaven-sent
assistance.

Is it not astounding that a city allows thousands of its youth to fill their impressionable
minds with these absurdities which certainly
will become the foundation for their working

moral codes and the data from which they will judge the proprieties of life?

It is as if a child, starved at home, should be forced to go out and search for food, selecting, quite naturally, not that which is nourishing but that which is exciting and appealing to his outward sense, often in his ignorance and foolishness blundering into substances which are filthy and poisonous.

Out of my twenty years' experience at Hull-House I can recall all sorts of pilferings, petty larcenies, and even burglaries, due to that never ceasing effort on the part of boys to procure theater tickets. I can also recall indirect efforts towards the same end which are most pitiful. I remember the remorse of a young girl of fifteen who was brought into the Juvenile Court after a night spent weeping in the cellar of her home because she had stolen a mass of artificial flowers with which to trim a hat. She stated that she had taken the flowers because she was afraid of losing the attention of a young man whom she had heard say that "a girl has to be dressy if she expects to be seen." This young man was the only one who had ever taken her to the theater and if he failed her, she was sure that she would never go again, and she sobbed out incoherently that she "couldn't live at all without it." Apparently the blankness and grayness of life itself had been broken for her only by the portrayal of a different world.

One boy whom I had known from babyhood began to take money from his mother from the time he was seven years old, and after he was ten she regularly gave him money for the play Saturday evening. However, the Saturday performance, "starting him off like," he always went twice again on Sunday, procuring the money in all sorts of illicit ways. Practically all of his earnings after he was fourteen were spent in this way to satisfy the insatiable desire to know of the great adventures of the wide world which the more fortunate boy takes out in reading Homer and Stevenson.

In talking with his mother, I was reminded of my experience one Sunday afternoon in Russia when the employees of a large factory were seated in an open-air theater, watching with breathless interest the presentation of folk stories. I was told that troupes of actors went from one manufacturing establishment to another presenting the simple elements of history and literature to the illiterate employees. This tendency to slake the thirst for adventure by viewing the drama is, of course, but a blind and primitive effort in the direction of culture, for "he who makes himself its vessel and bearer thereby acquires a freedom from the blindness and soul poverty of daily existence."

It is partly in response to this need that more sophisticated young people often go to the theater, hoping to find a clue to life's perplexities. Many times the bewildered hero reminds one of Emerson's description of Margaret Fuller, "I don't know where I am going, follow me"; nevertheless, the stage is dealing with the moral themes in which the public is most interested.

And while many young people go to the theater if only to see represented, and to hear discussed, the themes which seem to them so tragically important, there is no doubt that what they hear there, flimsy and poor as it often is, easily becomes their actual moral guide. In moments of moral crisis they turn to the sayings of the hero who found himself in a similar plight. The sayings may not be profound, but at least they are applicable to conduct. In the last few years scores of plays have been put upon the stage whose titles might be easily translated into proper headings for sociological lectures or sermons, without including the plays of Ibsen, Shaw and Hauptmann, which deal so directly with moral issues that the moralists themselves wince under their teachings and declare them brutal. But it is this very brutality which the over-refined and complicated city dwellers often crave. Moral teaching has become so intricate, creeds so metaphysical, that in a state of absolute reaction they demand definite instruction for daily living. Their whole-hearted acceptance of the teaching corroborates the statement recently made by an English playwright that "The theater is literally making the minds of our urban populations today. It is a huge factory of sentiment, of character, of points of honor, of conceptions of conduct, of everything that finally determines the destiny of a nation. The theater is not only a place of amusement, it is a place of culture, a place where people learn how to think, act, and feel." Seldom, however, do we associate the theater with our plans for civic righteousness, although it has become so important a factor in city life.

One Sunday evening last winter an investigation was made of four hundred and sixty six theaters in the city of Chicago, and it was discovered that in the majority of them the leading theme was revenge; the lover following his rival; the outraged husband seeking his wife's paramour; or the wiping out by death of a blot on a hitherto unstained honor. It was estimated that one sixth of the entire population of the city had attended the theaters on that day. At that same moment the churches throughout the city were preaching the gospel of good will. Is not this a striking commentary upon the contradictory influences to which the city youth is constantly subjected?

This discrepancy between the church and the stage is at times apparently recognized by the five-cent theater itself, and a blundering attempt is made to suffuse the songs and moving pictures with piety. Nothing could more absurdly demonstrate this attempt than a song, illustrated by pictures, describing the adventures of a young man who follows a pretty girl through street after street in the hope of "snatching a kiss from her ruby lips." The young man is overjoyed when a sudden wind storm drives the girl to shelter under an archway, and he is about to succeed in his attempt when the good Lord, "ever watchful over innocence," makes the same wind "blow a cloud of dust into the eyes of the rubberneck," and "his foul purpose is foiled." This attempt at piety is also shown in a series of films depicting Bible stories and the Passion Play at Oberammergau, forecasting the time when the moving film will be viewed as a mere mechanical device for the use of the church, the school and the library, as well as for the theater.

At present, however, most improbable tales hold the attention of the youth of the city night after night, and feed his starved imagination as nothing else succeeds in doing. In addition to these fascinations, the five-cent theater is also fast becoming the general social center and club house in many crowded neighborhoods. It is easy of access from the street, the entire family of parents and children can attend for a comparatively small sum of money, and the performance lasts for at least an hour; and, in some of the humbler theaters, the spectators are not disturbed for a second hour.

The room which contains the mimic stage is small and cozy, and less formal than the regular theater, and there is much more gossip and social life as if the foyer and pit were mingled. The very darkness of the room, necessary for an exhibition of the films, is an added attraction to many young people, for whom the space is filled with the glamour of love making.

Hundreds of young people attend these five-cent theaters every evening in the week, including Sunday, and what is seen and heard there becomes the sole topic of conversation, forming the ground pattern of their social life. That mutual understanding which in another social circle is provided by books, travel and all the arts, is here compressed into the topics suggested by the play.

The young people attend the five-cent

theaters in groups, with something of the
"gang" instinct, boasting of the films and
stunts in "our theater." They find a certain
advantage in attending one theater regularly,
for the *habitués* are often invited to come upon
the stage on "amateur nights," which occur
at least once a week in all the theaters. This
is, of course, a most exciting experience. If
the "stunt" does not meet with the approval
of the audience, the performer is greeted with
jeers and a long hook pulls him off the stage;
if, on the other hand, he succeeds in pleasing
the audience, he may be paid for his performance and later register with a booking agency,
the address of which is supplied by the obliging manager, and thus he fancies that a
lucrative and exciting career is opening before
him. Almost every night at six o'clock a long
line of children may be seen waiting at the
entrance of these booking agencies, of which
there are fifteen that are well known in
Chicago.

Thus, the only art which is constantly
placed before the eyes of "the temperamental
youth" is a debased form of dramatic art, and

a vulgar type of music, for the success of a song in these theaters depends not so much upon its musical rendition as upon the vulgarity of its appeal. In a song which held the stage of a cheap theater in Chicago for weeks, the young singer was helped out by a bit of mirror from which she threw a flash of light into the faces of successive boys whom she selected from the audience as she sang the refrain, "You are my Affinity." Many popular songs relate the vulgar experiences of a city man wandering from amusement park to bathing beach in search of flirtations. It may be that these "stunts" and recitals of city adventure contain the nucleus of coming poesy and romance, as the songs and recitals of the early minstrels sprang directly from the life of the people, but all the more does the effort need help and direction, both in the development of its technique and the material of its themes.

The few attempts which have been made in this direction are astonishingly rewarding to those who regard the power of self-expression as one of the most precious boons of education. The Children's Theater in New York is the

most successful example, but every settlement
in which dramatics have been systematically
fostered can also testify to a surprisingly
quick response to this form of art on the part
of young people. The Hull-House Theater is
constantly besieged by children clamoring to
"take part" in the plays of Schiller, Shakespeare, and Molière, although they know it
means weeks of rehearsal and the complete
memorizing of "stiff" lines. The audiences sit
enthralled by the final rendition and other
children whose tastes have supposedly been
debased by constant vaudeville, are patheti-
cally eager to come again and again. Even
when still more is required from the young
actors, research into the special historic period,
copying costumes from old plates, hours of
labor that the "th" may be restored to its
proper place in English speech, their enthusiasm is unquenched. But quite aside from its
educational possibilities one never ceases to
marvel at the power of even a mimic stage to
afford to the young a magic space in which
life may be lived in efflorescence, where man-
ners may be courtly and elaborate without

exciting ridicule, where the sequence of events is impressive and comprehensible. Order and beauty of life is what the adolescent youth craves above all else as the younger child indefatigably demands his story. "Is this where the most beautiful princess in the world lives?" asks a little girl peering into the door of the Hull-House Theater, or "Does Alice in Wonderland always stay here?" It is much easier for her to put her feeling into words than it is for the youth who has enchantingly rendered the gentle poetry of Ben Jonson's "Sad Shepherd," or for him who has walked the boards as Southey's Wat Tyler. His association, however, is quite as clinging and magical as is the child's although he can only say, "Gee, I wish I could always feel the way I did that night. Something would be doing then." Nothing of the artist's pleasure, nor of the revelation of that larger world which surrounds and completes our own, is lost to him because a careful technique has been exacted,—on the contrary this has only dignified and enhanced it. It would also be easy to illustrate youth's eagerness for artistic expression from the recitals given by the pupils of the New York Music School Settlement, or by those of the Hull-House Music School. These attempts also combine social life with the training of the artistic sense and in this approximate the fascinations of the five-cent theater.

This spring a group of young girls accustomed to the life of a five-cent theater, reluctantly refused an invitation to go to the country for a day's outing because the return on a late train would compel them to miss one evening's performance. They found it impossible to tear themselves away not only from the excitements of the theater itself but from the gaiety of the crowd of young men and girls invariably gathered outside discussing the sensational posters.

A steady English shopkeeper lately complained that unless he provided his four daughters with the money for the five-cent theaters every evening they would steal it from his till, and he feared that they might be driven to procure it in even more illicit ways. Because his entire family life had been thus disrupted he gloomily asserted that "this cheap show had ruined his 'ome and was the curse of America.'' This father was able to formulate the anxiety of many immigrant parents who are absolutely bewildered by the keen absorption of their children in the cheap theater. This anxiety is not, indeed, without foundation. An eminent alienist of Chicago states that he has had a number of patients among neurotic children whose emotional natures have been so over-wrought by the crude appeal to which they had been so constantly subjected in the theaters, that they have become victims of hallucination and mental disorder. The statement of this physician may be the first note of alarm which will awaken the city to its duty in regard to the theater, so that it shall at least be made safe and sane for the city child whose senses are already so abnormally developed.

This testimony of a physician that the conditions are actually pathological, may at last induce us to bestir ourselves in regard to procuring a more wholesome form of public recreation. Many efforts in social amelioration have been undertaken only after such exposures; in the meantime, while the occasional child is driven distraught, a hundred children permanently injure their eyes watching the moving films, and hundreds more seriously model their conduct upon the standards set before them on this mimic stage.

Three boys, aged nine, eleven and thirteen years, who had recently seen depicted the adventures of frontier life including the holding up of a stage coach and the lassoing of the driver, spent weeks planning to lasso, murder, and rob a neighborhood milkman, who started on his route at four o'clock in the morning. They made their headquarters in a barn and saved enough money to buy a revolver, adopting as their watchword the phrase "Dead Men Tell no Tales." One spring morning the conspirators, with their faces covered with black cloth, lay "in ambush" for the milkman. Fortunately for him, as the lariat was thrown the horse shied, and, although the shot was appropriately fired, the milkman's life was saved. Such a direct influence of the theater is by no means rare, even among older boys. Thirteen young lads were brought into the Municipal Court in Chicago during the first week that "Raffles, the Amateur Cracksman'' was upon the stage, each one with an outfit of burglar's tools in his possession, and each one shamefacedly admitting that the gentlemanly burglar in the play had suggested to him a career of similar adventure.

In so far as the illusions of the theater succeed in giving youth the rest and recreation which comes from following a more primitive code of morality, it has a close relation to the function performed by public games. It is, of course, less valuable because the sense of participation is largely confined to the emotions and the imagination, and does not involve the entire nature.

We might illustrate by the ''Wild West Show'' in which the onlooking boy imagines himself an active participant. The scouts, the Indians, the bucking ponies, are his real intimate companions and occupy his entire mind. In contrast with this we have the omnipresent game of tag which is, doubtless, also founded upon the chase. It gives the boy exercise and momentary echoes of the old excitement, but it is barren of suggestion and quickly degenerates into horse-play.

Well considered public games easily carried out in a park or athletic field, might both fill the mind with the imaginative material constantly supplied by the theater, and also afford the activity which the cramped muscles of the town dweller so sorely need. Even the unquestioned ability which the theater possesses to bring men together into a common mood and to afford them a mutual topic of conversation, is better accomplished with the one national game which we already possess, and might be infinitely extended through the organization of other public games.

The theater even now by no means competes with the baseball league games which are attended by thousands of men and boys who, during the entire summer, discuss the respective standing of each nine and the relative merits of every player. During the noon hour all the employees of a city factory gather in the nearest vacant lot to cheer their own home team in its practice for the next game with the nine of a neighboring manufacturing establishment and on a Saturday afternoon the entire male population of the city betakes itself to the baseball field; the ordinary means of transportation are supplemented by gay stage-coaches and huge automobiles, noisy with blowing horns and decked with gay pennants. The enormous crowd of cheering men and boys are talkative, good-natured, full of the holiday spirit, and absolutely released from the grind of life. They are lifted out of their individual affairs and so fused together that a man cannot tell whether it is his own shout or another's that fills his ears; whether it is his own coat or another's that he is wildly waving to celebrate a victory. He does not call the stranger who sits next to him his "brother" but he unconsciously embraces him in an overwhelming outburst of kindly feeling when the favorite player makes a home run. Does not this contain a suggestion of the undoubted power of public recreation to bring together all classes of a community in the modern city unhappily so full of devices for keeping men apart?

Already some American cities are making a beginning toward more adequate public recreation. Boston has its municipal gymnasiums, cricket fields, and golf grounds. Chicago has seventeen parks with playing fields, gymnasiums and baths, which at present enroll thousands of young people. These same parks are provided with beautiful halls which are used for many purposes, rent free, and are given over to any group of young people who wish to conduct dancing parties subject to city supervision and chaperonage. Many social clubs have deserted neighboring saloon halls for these municipal drawing rooms beautifully decorated with growing plants supplied by the park greenhouses, and flooded with electric lights supplied by the park power house. In the saloon halls the young people were obliged to ''pass money freely over the bar,'' and in order to make the most of the occasion they usually stayed until morning. At such times the economic necessity itself would override the counsels of the more temperate, and the thrifty door keeper would not insist upon invitations but would take in any one who had the ''price of a ticket.'' The free rent in the park hall, the good food in the park restaurant, supplied at cost, have made three parties closing at eleven o'clock no more expensive than one party breaking up at daylight, too often in disorder.

Is not this an argument that the drinking, the late hours, the lack of decorum, are directly traceable to the commercial enterprise which ministers to pleasure in order to drag it into excess because excess is more profitable? To thus commercialize pleasure is as monstrous as it is to commercialize art. It is intolerable that the city does not take over this function of making provision for pleasure, as wise communities in Sweden and South Carolina have taken the sale of alcohol out of the hands of enterprising publicans.

We are only beginning to understand what might be done through the festival, the street procession, the band of marching musicians, orchestral music in public squares or parks, with the magic power they all possess to formulate the sense of companionship and solidarity. The experiments which are being made in public schools to celebrate the national holidays, the changing seasons, the birthdays of heroes, the planting of trees, are slowly developing little ceremonials which may in time work out into pageants of genuine beauty and significance. No other nation has so unparalleled an opportunity to do this through its schools as we have, for no other nation has so wide-spreading a school system, while the enthusiasm of children and their natural ability to express their emotions through symbols, gives the securest possible foundation to this growing effort.

The city schools of New York have effected the organization of high school girls into groups for folk dancing. These old forms of dancing which have been worked out in many lands and through long experiences, safeguard unwary and dangerous expression and yet afford a vehicle through which the gaiety of youth may flow. Their forms are indeed those which lie at the basis of all good breeding, forms which at once express and restrain, urge forward and set limits.

One may also see another center of growth for public recreation and the beginning of a pageantry for the people in the many small parks and athletic fields which almost every

American city is hastening to provide for its young. These small parks have innumerable athletic teams, each with its distinctive uniform, with track meets and match games arranged with the teams from other parks and from the public schools; choruses of trade unionists or of patriotic societies fill the park halls with eager listeners. Labor Day processions are yearly becoming more carefully planned and more picturesque in character, as the desire to make an overwhelming impression with mere size gives way to a growing ambition to set forth the significance of the craft and the skill of the workman. At moments they almost rival the dignified showing of the processions of the German Turn Vereins which are also often seen in our city streets.

The many foreign colonies which are found in all American cities afford an enormous reserve of material for public recreation and street festival. They not only celebrate the feasts and holidays of the fatherland, but have each their own public expression for their mutual benefit societies and for the observance of American anniversaries. From the gay cele-

bration of the Scandinavians when war was
averted and two neighboring nations were
united, to the equally gay celebration of the
centenary of Garibaldi's birth; from the Chinese dragon cleverly trailing its way through
the streets, to the Greek banners flung out in
honor of immortal heroes, there is an infinite
variety of suggestions and possibilities for
public recreation and for the corporate expression of stirring emotions. After all, what is
the function of art but to preserve in permanent and beautiful form those emotions and
solaces which cheer life and make it kindlier,
more heroic and easier to comprehend; which
lift the mind of the worker from the harshness and loneliness of his task, and, by con-
necting him with what has gone before, free
him from a sense of isolation and hardship?

Were American cities really eager for municipal art, they would cherish as genuine beginnings the tarentella danced so interminably at
Italian weddings; the primitive Greek pipe
played throughout the long summer nights;
the Bohemian theaters crowded with eager
Slavophiles; the Hungarian musicians stroll-

ing from street to street; the fervid oratory of
the young Russian preaching social righteousness in the open square.

Many Chicago citizens who attended the first
annual meeting of the National Playground
Association of America, will never forget the
long summer day in the large playing field
filled during the morning with hundreds of
little children romping through the kindergarten games, in the afternoon with the young
men and girls contending in athletic sports;
and the evening light made gay by the bright
colored garments of Italians, Lithuanians, Nor-
wegians, and a dozen other nationalities, re-
producing their old dances and festivals for the
pleasure of the more stolid Americans. Was
this a forecast of what we may yet see accomplished through a dozen agencies promoting
public recreation which are springing up in
every city of America, as they already are
found in the large towns of Scotland and
England?

Let us cherish these experiments as the most
precious beginnings of an attempt to supply the
recreational needs of our industrial cities. To

fail to provide for the recreation of youth, is not only to deprive all of them of their natural form of expression, but is certain to subject some of them to the overwhelming temptation of illicit and soul-destroying pleasures. To insist that young people shall forecast their rose-colored future only in a house of dreams, is to deprive the real world of that warmth and reassurance which it so sorely needs and to which it is justly entitled; furthermore, we are left outside with a sense of dreariness, in company with that shadow which already lurks only around the corner for most of us—a skepticism of life's value.

CHAPTER V

THE SPIRIT OF YOUTH AND INDUSTRY

CHAPTER V

THE SPIRIT OF YOUTH AND INDUSTRY

As it is possible to establish a connection between the lack of public recreation and the vicious excitements and trivial amusements which become their substitutes, so it may be illuminating to trace the connection between the monotony and dullness of factory work and the petty immoralities which are often the youth's protest against them.

There are many city neighborhoods in which practically every young person who has attained the age of fourteen years enters a factory. When the work itself offers nothing of interest, and when no public provision is made for recreation, the situation becomes almost insupportable to the youth whose ancestors have been rough-working and hard-playing peasants.

In such neighborhoods the joy of youth is well nigh extinguished; and in that long procession of factory workers, each morning and evening, the young walk almost as wearily and listlessly as the old. Young people working in modern factories situated in cities still dominated by the ideals of Puritanism face a combination which tends almost irresistably to overwhelm the spirit of youth. When the Puritan repression of pleasure was in the ascendant in America the people it dealt with lived on farms and villages where, although youthful pleasures might be frowned upon and crushed out, the young people still had a chance to find self-expression in their work. Plowing the field and spinning the flax could be carried on with a certain joyousness and vigor which the organization of modern industry too often precludes. Present industry based upon the inventions of the nineteenth century has little connection with the old patterns in which men have worked for generations. The modern factory calls for an expenditure of nervous energy almost more than it demands muscular effort, or at least machinery so far performs the work of the massive muscles, that greater stress is laid upon fine and exact movements necessarily involving nervous strain. But these movements are exactly of the type to which the muscles of a growing boy least readily respond, quite as the admonition to be accurate and faithful is that which appeals the least to his big primitive emotions. The demands made upon his eyes are complicated and trivial, the use of his muscles is fussy and monotonous, the relation between cause and effect is remote and obscure. Apparently nc one is concerned as to what may be done to aid him in this process and to relieve it of its dullness and difficulty, to mitigate its strain and harshness.

Perhaps never before have young people been expected to work from motives so detached from direct emotional incentive. Never has the age of marriage been so long delayed; never has the work of youth been so separated from the family life and the public opinion of the community. Education alone can repair these losses. It alone has the power of organizing a child's activities with some reference to the life he will later lead and of giving him a clue as to what to select and what to eliminate when he comes into contact with contemporary social and industrial conditions. And until educators take hold of the situation, the rest of the community is powerless.

In vast regions of the city which are completely dominated by the factory, it is as if the development of industry had outrun all the educational and social arrangements.

The revolt of youth against uniformity and the necessity of following careful directions laid down by some one else, many times results in such nervous irritability that the youth, in spite of all sorts of prudential reasons, "throws up his job," if only to get outside the factory walls into the freer street, just as the narrowness of the school inclosure induces many a boy to jump the fence.

When the boy is on the street, however, and is "standing around on the corner" with the gang to which he mysteriously attaches himself, he finds the difficulties of direct untrammeled action almost as great there as they were in the factory, but for an entirely different set of reasons. The necessity so strongly felt in the factory for an outlet to his sudden and furious bursts of energy, his overmastering desire to prove that he could do things "without being bossed all the time," finds little chance for expression, for he discovers that in whatever really active pursuit he tries to engage, he is promptly suppressed by the police. After several futile attempts at self-expression, he returns to his street corner subdued and so far discouraged that when he has the next impulse to vigorous action he concludes that it is of no use, and sullenly settles back into inactivity. He thus learns to persuade himself that it is better to do nothing, or, as the psychologist would say, "to inhibit his motor impulses."

When the same boy, as an adult workman, finds himself confronted with an unusual or an untoward condition in his work, he will fall back into this habit of inhibition, of making no effort toward independent action. When "slack times" come, he will be the workman of least value, and the first to be dismissed, calmly accepting his position in the ranks of the unemployed because it will not be so unlike the many hours of idleness and vacuity to which he was accustomed as a boy. No help having been extended to him in the moment of his first

irritable revolt against industry, his whole life
has been given a twist toward idleness and
futility. He has not had the chance of recovery
which the school system gives a like rebellious
boy in a truant school.

The unjustifiable lack of educational supervision during the first years of factory work
makes it quite impossible for the modern educator to offer any real assistance to young
people during that trying transitional period
between school and industry. The young people themselves who fail to conform can do little
but rebel against the entire situation, and the
expressions of revolt roughly divide themselves
into three classes. The first, resulting in idleness, may be illustrated from many a sad story
of a boy or a girl who has spent in the first spurt
of premature and uninteresting work, all the
energy which should have carried them through
years of steady endeavor.

I recall a boy who had worked steadily for
two years as a helper in a smelting establishment, and had conscientiously brought home
all his wages, one night suddenly announcing
to his family that he "was too tired and too

hot to go on.'' As no amount of persuasion
could make him alter his decision, the family
finally threatened to bring him into the Juvenile Court on a charge of incorrigibility, whereupon the boy disappeared and such efforts as
the family have been able to make in the two
years since, have failed to find him. They are
convinced that ''he is trying a spell of tramp-
ing'' and wish that they ''had let him have a
vacation the first summer when he wanted it so
bad.'' The boy may find in the rough outdoor life the healing which a wise physician
would recommend for nervous exhaustion, although the tramp experiment is a perilous one.

This revolt against factory monotony is sometimes closely allied to that ''moral fatigue''
which results from assuming responsibility
prematurely. I recall the experience of a Scotch
girl of eighteen who, with her older sister,
worked in a candy factory, their combined
earnings supporting a paralytic father. The
older girl met with an accident involving the
loss of both eyes, and the financial support of
the whole family devolved upon the younger
girl, who worked hard and conscientiously for

three years, supplementing her insufficient factory wages by evening work at glove making. In the midst of this devotion and monotonous existence she made the acquaintance of a girl who was a chorus singer in a cheap theater and the contrast between her monotonous drudgery and the glitter of the stage broke down her allegiance to her helpless family. She left the city, absolutely abandoning the kindred to whom she had been so long devoted, and announced that if they all starved she would "never go into a factory again." Every effort failed to find her after the concert troupe left Milwaukee and although the pious Scotch father felt that "she had been ensnared by the Devil," and had brought his "gray hairs in sorrow to the grave," I could not quite dismiss the case with this simple explanation, but was haunted by all sorts of social implications.

The second line of revolt manifests itself in an attempt to make up for the monotony of the work by a constant change from one occupation to another. This is an almost universal experience among thousands of young people in their first impact with the industrial world.

The startling results of the investigation undertaken in Massachusetts by the Douglas Commission showed how casual and demoralizing the first few years of factory life become to thousands of unprepared boys and girls; in their first restlessness and maladjustment they change from one factory to another, working only for a few weeks or months in each, and they exhibit no interest in any of them save for the amount of wages paid. At the end of their second year of employment many of them are less capable than when they left school and are actually receiving less wages. The report of the commission made clear that while the two years between fourteen and sixteen were most valuable for educational purposes, they were almost useless for industrial purposes, that no trade would receive as an apprentice a boy under sixteen, that no industry requiring skill and workmanship could utilize these untrained children and that they not only demoralized themselves, but in a sense industry itself.

An investigation of one thousand tenement

children in New York who had taken out their "working papers" at the age of fourteen, reported that during the first working year a third of them had averaged six places each. These reports but confirm the experience of those of us who live in an industrial neighborhood and who continually see these restless young workers, in fact there are moments when this constant changing seems to be all that saves them from the fate of those other children who hold on to a monotonous task so long that they finally incapacitate themselves for all work.   It often seems to me an expression of the instinct of self-preservation, as in the case of a young Swedish boy who during a period of two years abandoned one piece of factory work after another, saying "he could not stand it," until in the chagrin following the loss of his ninth place he announced his intention of leaving the city and allowing his mother and little sisters to shift for themselves.   At this critical juncture a place was found for him as lineman in a telephone company; climbing telephone poles and handling wires apparently supplied him with the elements of outdoor activity and danger which were necessary to hold his interest, and he became the steady support of his family.

But while we know the discouraging effect of idleness upon the boy who has thrown up his job and refuses to work again, and we also know the restlessness and lack of discipline resulting from the constant change from one factory to another, there is still a third manifestation of maladjustment of which one's memory and the Juvenile Court records unfortunately furnish many examples. The spirit of revolt in these cases has led to distinct disaster. Two stories will perhaps be sufficient in illustration although they might be multiplied indefinitely from my own experience.

A Russian girl who went to work at an early age in a factory, pasting labels on mucilage bottles, was obliged to surrender all her wages to her father who, in return, gave her only the barest necessities of life. In a fit of revolt against the monotony of her work, and "that nasty sticky stuff," she stole from her father $300 which he had hidden away under the floor of his kitchen, and with this money she ran away to a neighboring city for a spree, having first bought herself the most gorgeous clothing a local department store could supply. Of course, this preposterous beginning could have but one ending and the child was sent to the reform school to expiate not only her own sins but the sins of those who had failed to rescue her from a life of grinding monotony which her spirit could not brook.

"I know the judge thinks I am a bad girl," sobbed a poor little prisoner, put under bonds for threatening to kill her lover, "but I have only been bad for one week and before that I was good for six years. I worked every day in Blank's factory and took home all my wages to keep the kids in school. I met this fellow in a dance hall. I just had to go to dances sometimes after pushing down the lever of my machine with my right foot and using both my arms feeding it for ten hours a day—nobody knows how I felt some nights. I agreed to go away with this man for a week but when I was ready to go home he tried to drive me out on the street to earn money for him and, of course, I threatened to kill him—any decent girl would," she concluded, as unconscious of the irony of the reflection as she was of the connection between her lurid week and her monotonous years.

Knowing as educators do that thousands of the city youth will enter factory life at an age as early as the state law will permit; instructed as the modern teacher is as to youth's requirements for a normal mental and muscular development, it is hard to understand the apathy in regard to youth's inevitable experience in modern industry. Are the educators, like the rest of us, so caught in admiration of the astonishing achievements of modern industry that they forget the children themselves?

A Scotch educator who recently visited America considered it very strange that with a remarkable industrial development all about us, affording such amazing educational opportunities, our schools should continually cling to a past which did not fit the American temperament, was not adapted to our needs, and made no vigorous pull upon our faculties. He concluded that our educators, overwhelmed by the size and vigor of American industry, were too timid to seize upon the industrial situation and to extract its enormous educational value. He lamented that this lack of courage and initiative failed not only to fit the child for an intelligent and conscious participation in industrial life, but that it was reflected in the industrial development itself; that industry had fallen back into old habits, and repeated traditional mistakes until American cities exhibited stupendous extensions of the medievalisms in the traditional Ghetto, and of the hideousness in the Black Country of Lancashire.

He contended that this condition is the inevitable result of separating education from contemporary life. Education becomes unreal and far fetched, while industry becomes ruthless and materialistic. In spite of the severity of the indictment, one much more severe and well deserved might have been brought against us. He might have accused us not only of wasting, but of misusing and of trampling under foot the first tender instincts and impulses which are the source of all charm and beauty and art, because we fail to realize that by premature factory work, for which the youth is unprepared, society perpetually extinguishes that variety and promise, that bloom of life, which is the unique possession of the young. He might have told us that our cities would continue to be traditionally cramped and dreary until we comprehend that youth alone has the power to bring to reality the vision of the "Coming City of Mankind, full of life, full of the spirit of creation."

A few educational experiments are carried on in Cincinnati, in Boston and in Chicago, in which the leaders of education and industry unite in a common aim and purpose. A few more are carried on by trade unionists, who in at least two of the trades are anxious to give to their apprentices and journeymen the wider culture afforded by the "capitalistic trade schools" which they suspect of preparing strike-breakers; still a few other schools have been founded by public spirited citizens to whom the situation has become unendurable, and one or two more such experiments are attached to the public school system itself. All of these schools are still blundering in method and unsatisfactory in their results, but a certain trade school for girls, in New York, which is preparing young girls of fourteen for the sewing trade, already so overcrowded and subdivided that there remains very little education for the worker, is conquering this difficult industrial situation by equipping each apprentice with "the informing mind." If a child goes into a sewing factory with a knowledge of the work she is doing in relation to the finished product; if she is informed concerning the material she is manipulating and the processes to which it is subjected; if she understands the design she is elaborating in its historic relation to art and decoration, her daily life is lifted from drudgery to one of self-conscious activity, and her pleasure and intelligence is registered in her product.

I remember a little colored girl in this New York school who was drawing for the pattern she was about to embroider, a carefully elaborated acanthus leaf. Upon my inquiry as to the design, she replied: "It is what the Egyptians used to put on everything, because they saw it so much growing in the Nile; and then the Greeks copied it, and sometimes you

can find it now on the buildings downtown.''
She added, shyly: ''Of course, I like it awfully
well because it was first used by people living
in Africa where the colored folks come from.''
Such a reasonable interest in work not only
reacts upon the worker, but is, of course, registered in the product itself.   Such genuine
pleasure is in pitiful contrast to the usual manifestation of the play spirit as it is found in
the factories, where, at the best, its expression
is illicit and often is attended with great danger.

There are many touching stories by which
this might be illustrated.   One of them comes
from a large steel mill of a boy of fifteen whose
business it was to throw a lever when a small
tank became filled with molton metal.   During the few moments when the tank was filling
it was his foolish custom to catch the reflection
of the metal upon a piece of looking-glass, and
to throw the bit of light into the eyes of
his fellow workmen.   Although an exasperated
foreman had twice dispossessed him of his
mirror, with a third fragment he was one day
flicking the gloom of the shop when the neglected tank overflowed, almost instantly burn-

ing off both his legs. Boys working in the stock yards, during their moments of wrestling and rough play, often slash each other painfully with the short knives which they use in their work, but in spite of this the play impulse is too irrepressible to be denied.

If educators could go upon a voyage of discovery into that army of boys and girls who enter industry each year, what values might they not discover; what treasures might they not conserve and develop if they would direct the play instinct into the art impulse and utilize that power of variation which industry so sadly needs. No force will be sufficiently powerful and widespread to redeem industry from its mechanism and materialism save the freed power in every single individual.

In order to do this, however, we must go back a little over the educational road to a training of the child's imagination, as well as to his careful equipment with a technique. A little child makes a very tottering house of cardboard and calls it a castle. The important feature there lies in the fact that he has expressed a castle, and it is not for his teacher to draw undue attention to the fact that the corners are not well put together, but rather to listen to and to direct the story which centers about this effort at creative expression. A little later, however, it is clearly the business of the teacher to call attention to the quality of the dovetailing in which the boy at the manual training bench is engaged, for there is no value in dovetailing a box unless it is accurately done. At one point the child's imagination is to be emphasized, and at another point his technique is important—and he will need both in the industrial life ahead of him.

There is no doubt that there is a third period, when the boy is not interested in the making of a castle, or a box, or anything else, unless it appears to him to bear a direct relation to the future; unless it has something to do with earning a living. At this later moment he is chiefly anxious to play the part of a man and to take his place in the world. The fact that a boy at fourteen wants to go out and earn his living makes that the moment when he should be educated with reference to that interest, and the records of many high schools show that if he is not thus educated, he bluntly refuses to be educated at all. The forces pulling him to "work" are not only the over-mastering desire to earn money and be a man, but, if the family purse is small and empty, include also his family loyalty and affection, and over against them, we at present place nothing but a vague belief on the part of his family and himself that education is a desirable thing and may eventually help him "on in the world." It is of course difficult to adapt education to this need; it means that education must be planned so seriously and definitely for those two years between fourteen and six-teen that it will be actual trade training so far as it goes, with attention given to the condition under which money will be actually paid for industrial skill; but at the same time, that the implications, the connections, the relations to the industrial world, will be made clear. A man who makes, year after year, but one small wheel in a modern watch factory, may, if his education has properly prepared him, have a fuller life than did the old watchmaker who made a watch from beginning to end. It takes thirty-nine people to make a coat in a modern tailoring establishment, yet those same thirty-nine people might produce a coat in a spirit of "team work" which would make the entire process as much more exhilarating than the work of the old solitary tailor, as playing in a baseball nine gives more pleasure to a boy than that afforded by a solitary game of hand ball on the side of the barn. But it is quite impossible to imagine a successful game of baseball in which each player should be drilled only in his own part, and should know nothing of the relation of that part to the whole game. In order to make the watch wheel, or the coat collar interesting, they must be connected with the entire product—must include fellowship as well as the pleasures arising from skilled workmanship and a cultivated imagination.

When all the young people working in factories shall come to use their faculties intelligently, and as a matter of course to be interested in what they do, then our manufactured products may at last meet the demands of a cultivated nation, because they will be produced by cultivated workmen. The machine will not be abandoned by any means, but will be subordinated to the intelligence of the man who manipulates it, and will be used as a tool. It may come about in time that an educated public will become inexpressibly bored by manufactured objects which reflect absolutely nothing of the minds of the men who made them, that they may come to dislike an object made by twelve unrelated men, even as we do not care for a picture which has been painted by a dozen different men, not because we have enunciated a theory in regard to it, but because such a picture loses all its significance and has no meaning or message. We need to apply the same principle but very little further until we shall refuse to be surrounded by manufactured objects which do not represent some gleam of intelligence on the part of the producer. Hundreds of people have already taken that step so far as all decoration and ornament are concerned, and it would require but one short step more. In the meantime we are surrounded by stupid articles which give us no pleasure, and the

young people producing them are driven into
all sorts of expedients in order to escape work
which has been made impossible because all
human interest has been extracted from it.
That this is not mere theory may be demon-
strated by the fact that many times the young
people may be spared the disastrous effects
of this third revolt against the monotony of
industry if work can be found for them in a
place where the daily round is less grinding
and presents more variety. Fortunately, in
every city there are places outside of factories
where occupation of a more normal type of
labor may be secured, and often a restless boy
can be tided over this period if he is put into
one of these occupations. The experience in
every boys' club can furnish illustrations of
this.

A factory boy who had been brought into
the Juvenile Court many times because of his
persistent habit of borrowing the vehicles of
physicians as they stood in front of houses of
patients, always meaning to "get back before
the doctor came out," led a contented and
orderly life after a place had been found for

him as a stable boy in a large livery establishment where his love for horses could be legitimately gratified.

Still another boy made the readjustment for himself in spite of the great physical suffering involved. He had lost both legs at the age of seven, "flipping cars." When he went to work at fourteen with two good cork legs, which he vainly imagined disguised his disability, his employer kindly placed him where he might sit throughout the entire day, and his task was to keep tally on the boxes constantly hoisted from the warehouse into cars. The boy found this work so dull that he insisted upon working in the yards, where the cars were being loaded and switched. He would come home at night utterly exhausted, more from the extreme nervous tension involved in avoiding accidents than from the tremendous exertion, and although he would weep bitterly from sheer fatigue, nothing could induce him to go back to the duller and safer job. Fortunately he belonged to a less passionate race than the poor little Italian girl in the Hull-House neighborhood who recently battered her

head against the wall so long and so vigorously
that she had to be taken to a hospital because
of her serious injuries. So nearly as dull
"grown-ups" could understand, it had been an
hysterical revolt against factory work by day
and "no fun in the evening."

America perhaps more than any other country in the world can demonstrate what applied
science has accomplished for industry; it has
not only made possible the utilization of all
sorts of unpromising raw material, but it has
tremendously increased the invention and
elaboration of machinery. The time must come,
however, if indeed the moment has not already
arrived, when applied science will have done
all that it can do for the development of
machinery. It may be that machines cannot
be speeded up any further without putting
unwarranted strain upon the nervous system
of the worker; it may be that further elaboration will so sacrifice the workman who feeds
the machine that industrial advance will lie
not in the direction of improvement in machinery, but in the recovery and education of
the workman. This refusal to apply "the art

of life" to industry continually drives out of
it many promising young people. Some of
them, impelled by a creative impulse which
will not be denied, avoid industry altogether
and demand that their ambitious parents give
them lessons in "china painting" and "art
work," which clutters the overcrowded parlor
of the more prosperous workingman's home
with useless decorated plates, and handpainted
"drapes," whereas the plates upon the table
and the rugs upon the floor used daily by
thousands of weary housewives are totally un-
touched by the beauty and variety which this
ill-directed art instinct might have given them
had it been incorporated into industry.

I could cite many instances of high-spirited
young people who suffer a veritable martyrdom
in order to satisfy their artistic impulse.

A young girl of fourteen whose family had
for years displayed a certain artistic aptitude,
the mother having been a singer and the grand-
mother, with whom the young girl lived, a
clever worker in artificial flowers, had her first
experience of wage earning in a box factory.
She endured it only for three months, and then

gave up her increasing wage in exchange for $1.50 a week which she earns by making sketches of dresses, cloaks and hats for the advertisements of a large department store.

A young Russian girl of my acquaintance starves on the irregular pay which she receives for her occasional contributions to the Sunday newspapers—meanwhile writing her novel— rather than return to the comparatively prosperous wages of a necktie factory which she regards with horror. Another girl washes dishes every evening in a cheap boarding house in order to secure the leisure in which to practise her singing lessons, rather than to give them up and return to her former twelve-dollar-a-week job in an electrical factory.

The artistic expression in all these cases is crude, but the young people are still conscious of that old sacrifice of material interest which art has ever demanded of those who serve her and which doubtless brings its own reward. That the sacrifice is in vain makes it all the more touching and is an indictment of the educator who has failed to utilize the art instinct in industry.

Something of the same sort takes place among many lads who find little opportunity in the ordinary factories to utilize the "instinct for workmanship"; or, among those more prosperous young people who establish "studios" and "art shops," in which, with a vast expenditure of energy, they manufacture luxurious articles.

The educational system in Germany is deliberately planned to sift out and to retain in the service of industry, all such promising young people. The method is as yet experimental, and open to many objections, but it is so far successful that "Made in Germany" means made by a trained artisan and in many cases by a man working with the freed impulse of the artist.

The London County Council is constantly urging plans which may secure for the gifted children in the Board Schools support in Technological institutes. Educators are thus gradually developing the courage and initiative to conserve for industry the young worker himself so that his mind, his power of variation, his art instinct, his intelligent skill, may ultimately be reflected in the industrial product. That would imply that industry must be seized upon and conquered by those educators, who now either avoid it altogether by taking refuge in the caves of classic learning or beg the question by teaching the tool industry advocated by Ruskin and Morris in their first reaction against the present industrial system. It would mean that educators must bring industry into "the kingdom of the mind"; and pervade it with the human spirit.

The discovery of the labor power of youth was to our age like the discovery of a new natural resource, although it was merely incidental to the invention of modern machinery and the consequent subdivision of labor. In utilizing it thus ruthlessly we are not only in danger of quenching the divine fire of youth, but we are imperiling industry itself when we venture to ignore these very sources of beauty, of variety and of suggestion.

CHAPTER VI

THE THIRST FOR RIGHTEOUSNESS

CHAPTER VI

THE THIRST FOR RIGHTEOUSNESS

Even as we pass by the joy and beauty of youth on the streets without dreaming it is there, so we may hurry past the very presence of august things without recognition. We may easily fail to sense those spiritual realities, which, in every age, have haunted youth and called to him without ceasing. Historians tell us that the extraordinary advances in human progress have been made in those times when "the ideals of freedom and law, of youth and beauty, of knowledge and virtue, of humanity and religion, high things, the conflicts between which have caused most of the disruptions and despondences of human society, seem for a generation or two to lie in the same direction."

Are we perhaps at least twice in life's journey dimly conscious of the needlessness of this disruption and of the futility of the despondency? Do we feel it first when young ourselves

139

we long to interrogate the "transfigured few"
among our elders whom we believe to be carrying
forward affairs of gravest import? Failing
to accomplish this are we, for the second time,
dogged by a sense of lost opportunity, of need-
less waste and perplexity, when we too, as
adults, see again the dreams of youth in conflict
with the efforts of our own contemporaries?
We see idealistic endeavor on the one hand
lost in ugly friction; the heat and burden of
the day borne by mature men and women on
the other hand, increased by their consciousness
of youth's misunderstanding and high scorn.
It may relieve the mind to break forth in moments of irritation against "the folly of the
coming generation," but whoso pauses on his
plodding way to call even his youngest and
rashest brother a fool, ruins thereby the joy of
his journey,—for youth is so vivid an element
in life that unless it is cherished, all the rest is
spoiled. The most praiseworthy journey grows
dull and leaden unless companioned by youth's
iridescent dreams. Not only that, but the
mature of each generation run a grave risk of
putting their efforts in a futile direction, in a

blind alley as it were, unless they can keep in touch with the youth of their own day and know at least the trend in which eager dreams are driving them—those dreams that fairly buffet our faces as we walk the city streets.

At times every one possessed with a concern for social progress is discouraged by the formless and unsubdued modern city, as he looks upon that complicated life which drives men almost without their own volition, that life of ingenuous enterprises, great ambitions, political jealousies, where men tend to become mere "slaves of possessions." Doubtless these striving men are full of weakness and sensitiveness even when they rend each other, and are but caught in the coils of circumstance; nevertheless, a serious attempt to ennoble and enrich the content of city life that it may really fill the ample space their ruthless wills have provided, means that we must call upon energies other than theirs. When we count over the resources which are at work "to make order out of casualty, beauty out of confusion, justice, kindliness and mercy out of cruelty and inconsiderate pressure," we find ourselves appealing

to the confident spirit of youth. We know
that it is crude and filled with conflicting
hopes, some of them unworthy and most of
them doomed to disappointment, yet these
young people have the advantage of "morning
in their hearts"; they have such power of direct action, such ability to stand free from
fear, to break through life's trammelings, that
in spite of ourselves we become convinced that

"They to the disappointed earth shall give
The lives we meant to live."

That this solace comes to us only in fugitive
moments, and is easily misleading, may be
urged as an excuse for our blindness and in-
sensitiveness to the august moral resources
which the youth of each city offers to those
who are in the midst of the city's turmoil. A
further excuse is afforded in the fact that the
form of the dreams for beauty and righteousness change with each generation and that
while it is always difficult for the fathers to
understand the sons, at those periods when the
demand of the young is one of social reconstruction, the misunderstanding easily grows
into bitterness.

The old desire to achieve, to improve the world, seizes the ardent youth to-day with a stern command to bring about juster social conditions. Youth's divine impatience with the world's inheritance of wrong and injustice makes him scornful of "rose water for the plague" prescriptions, and he insists upon something strenuous and vital.

One can find innumerable illustrations of this idealistic impatience with existing conditions among the many Russian subjects found in the foreign quarters of every American city. The idealism of these young people might be utilized to a modification of our general culture and point of view, somewhat as the influence of the young Germans who came to America in the early fifties, bringing with them the hopes and aspirations embodied in the revolutions of 1848, made a profound impression upon the social and political institutions of America. Long before they emigrated, thousands of Russian young people had been caught up into the excitements and hopes of the Russian revolution in Finland, in Poland, in the Russian cities, in the university towns. Life

had become intensified by the consciousness
of the suffering and starvation of millions of
their fellow subjects. They had been living
with a sense of discipline and of preparation
for a coming struggle which, although grave
in import, was vivid and adventurous. Their
minds had been seized by the first crude forms
of social theory and they had cherished a vague
belief that they were the direct instruments
of a final and ideal social reconstruction. When
they come to America they sadly miss this sense
of importance and participation in a great and
glorious conflict against a recognized enemy.
Life suddenly grows stale and unprofitable; the
very spirit of tolerance which characterizes
American cities is that which strikes most un-
bearably upon their ardent spirits. They look
upon the indifference all about them with an
amazement which rapidly changes to irritation.
Some of them in a short time lose their ardor,
others with incredible rapidity make the adapta-
tion between American conditions and their
store of enthusiasm, but hundreds of them remain restless and ill at ease. Their only con-
solation, almost their only real companionship,

is when they meet in small groups for discussion
or in larger groups to welcome a well known
revolutionist who brings them direct news from
the conflict, or when they arrange for a demon-
stration in memory of "The Red Sunday" or
the death of Gershuni. Such demonstrations,
however, are held in honor of men whose sense
of justice was obliged to seek an expression quite
outside the regular channels of established government. Knowing that Russia has forced
thousands of her subjects into this position,
one would imagine that patriotic teachers in
America would be most desirous to turn into
governmental channels all that insatiable desire for juster relations in industrial and
political affairs. A distinct and well directed
campaign is necessary if this gallant enthusiasm is ever to be made part of that old and
still incomplete effort to embody in law—"the
law that abides and falters not, ages long"—the
highest aspirations for justice.

Unfortunately, we do little or nothing with
this splendid store of youthful ardor and creative enthusiasm. Through its very isolation it
tends to intensify and turn in upon itself, and

no direct effort is made to moralize it, to discipline it, to make it operative upon the life of the city. And yet it is, perhaps, what American cities need above all else, for it is but too true that Democracy—"a people ruling"—the very name of which the Greeks considered so beautiful, no longer stirs the blood of the American youth, and that the real enthusiasm for self-government must be found among the groups of young immigrants who bring over with every ship a new cargo of democratic aspirations. That many of these young men look for a consummation of these aspirations to a social order of the future in which the industrial system as well as government shall embody democratic relations, simply shows that the doctrine of Democracy like any other of the living faiths of men, is so essentially mystical that it continually demands new formulation. To fail to recognize it in a new form, to call it hard names, to refuse to receive it, may mean to reject that which our fathers cherished and handed on as an inheritance not only to be preserved but also to be developed.

We allow a great deal of this precious stuff—

this *Welt-Schmerz* of which each generation has need—not only to go unutilized, but to work havoc among the young people themselves. One of the saddest illustrations of this, in my personal knowledge, was that of a young Russian girl who lived with a group of her compatriots on the west side of Chicago. She recently committed suicide at the same time that several others in the group tried it and failed. One of these latter, who afterwards talked freely of the motives which led her to this act, said that there were no great issues at stake in this country; that America was wholly commercial in its interests and absorbed in money making; that Americans were not held together by any historic bonds nor great mutual hopes, and were totally ignorant of the stirring social and philosophic movements of Europe; that her life here had been a long, dreary, economic struggle, unrelieved by any of the higher interests; that she was tired of getting seventy-five cents for trimming a hat that sold for twelve dollars and was to be put upon the empty head of some one who had no concern for the welfare of the woman who

made it. The statement doubtless reflected
something of "The Sorrows of Werther," but
the entire tone was nobler and more highly
socialized.

It is difficult to illustrate what might be
accomplished by reducing to action the ardor
of those youths who so bitterly arraign our
present industrial order. While no part of
the social system can be changed rapidly, we
would all admit that the present industrial
arrangements in America might be vastly im-
proved and that we are failing to meet the requirements of our industrial life with courage
and success simply because we do not realize
that unless we establish that humane legislation which has its roots in a consideration for
human life, our industrialism itself will suffer
from inbreeding, growing ever more unrestrained and ruthless. It would seem obvious
that in order to secure relief in a community
dominated by industrial ideals, an appeal must
be made to the old spiritual sanctions for
human conduct, that we must reach motives
more substantial and enduring than the mere
fleeting experiences of one phase of modern

industry which vainly imagines that its growth would be curtailed if the welfare of its employees were guarded by the state. It would be an interesting attempt to turn that youthful enthusiasm to the aid of one of the most conservative of the present social efforts, the almost world-wide movement to secure protective legislation for women and children in industry, in which America is so behind the other nations. Fourteen of the great European powers protect women from all night work, from excessive labor by day, because paternalistic governments prize the strength of women for the bearing and rearing of healthy children to the state. And yet in a republic it is the citizens themselves who must be convinced of the need of this protection unless they would permit industry to maim the very mothers of the future.

In one year in the German Empire one hundred thousand children were cared for through money paid from the State Insurance fund to their widowed mothers or to their invalided fathers. And yet in the American states it seems impossible to pass a most rudimentary employers' liability act, which would be but the first step towards that code of beneficent legislation which protects "the widow and fatherless" in Germany and England. Certainly we shall have to bestir ourselves if we would care for the victims of the industrial order as well as do other nations. We shall be obliged speedily to realize that in order to secure protective legislation from a governmental body in which the most powerful interests represented are those of the producers and transporters of manufactured goods, it will be necessary to exhort to a care for the defenseless from the religious point of view. To take even the non-commercial point of view would be to assert that evolutionary progress assumes that a sound physique is the only secure basis of life, and to guard the mothers of the race is simple sanity.

And yet from lack of preaching we do not unite for action because we are not stirred to act at all, and protective legislation in America is shamefully inadequate. Because it is always difficult to put the championship of the oppressed above the counsels of prudence, we say in despair sometimes that we are a people who hold such varied creeds that there are not enough of one religious faith to secure anything, but the truth is that it is easy to unite for action people whose hearts have once been filled by the fervor of that willing devotion which may easily be generated in the youthful breast. It is comparatively easy to enlarge a moral concept, but extremely difficult to give it to an adult for the first time. And yet when we attempt to appeal to the old sanctions for disinterested conduct, the conclusion is often forced upon us that they have not been engrained into character, that they cannot be relied upon when they are brought into contact with the arguments of industrialism, that the colors of the flag flying over the fort of our spiritual resources wash out and disappear when the storm actually breaks.

It is because the ardor of youth has not been attracted to the long effort to modify the ruthlessness of industry by humane enactments, that we sadly miss their resourceful enthusiasm and that at the same time groups of young people who hunger and thirst after social righteousness are breaking their hearts because the social reform is so long delayed and an unsympathetic and hardhearted society frustrates all their hopes. And yet these ardent young people who obscure the issue by their crying and striving and looking in the wrong place, might be of inestimable value if so-called political leaders were in any sense social philosophers. To permit these young people to separate themselves from the contemporaneous efforts of ameliorating society and to turn their vague hopes solely toward an ideal commonwealth of the future, is to withdraw from an experimental self-government founded in enthusiasm, the very stores of enthusiasm which are needed to sustain it.

The championship of the oppressed came to be a spiritual passion with the Hebrew prophets. They saw the promises of religion, not for individuals but in the broad reaches of national affairs and in the establishment of social justice. It is quite possible that such a spiritual passion is again to be found among the ardent young souls of our cities. They see a vision, not of a purified nation but of a regenerated and a reorganized society. Shall we throw all this into the future, into the futile prophecy of those who talk because they cannot achieve, or shall we commingle their ardor, their overmastering desire for social justice, with that more sober effort to modify existing conditions? Are we once more forced to appeal to the educators? Is it so difficult to utilize this ardor because educators have failed to apprehend the spiritual quality of their task?

It would seem a golden opportunity for those to whom is committed the task of spiritual instruction, for to preach and seek justice in human affairs is one of the oldest obligations of religion and morality. All that would be necessary would be to attach this teaching to the contemporary world in such wise that the eager youth might feel a tug upon his faculties, and a sense of participation in the moral life about him. To leave it unattached to actual social movements means that the moralist is speaking in incomprehensible terms. Without this connection, the religious teachers may have conscientiously carried out their traditional duties and yet have failed utterly to stir the fires of spiritual enthusiasm.

Each generation of moralists and educators find themselves facing an inevitable dilemma; first, to keep the young committed to their charge "unspotted from the world," and, second, to connect the young with the ruthless and materialistic world all about them in such wise that they may make it the arena for their spiritual endeavor. It is fortunate for these teachers that sometime during "The Golden Age" the most prosaic youth is seized by a new interest in remote and universal ends, and that if but given a clue by which he may connect his lofty aims with his daily living, he himself will drag the very heavens into the most sordid tenement. The perpetual difficulty consists in finding the clue for him and placing it in his hands, for, if the teaching is too detached from life, it does not result in any psychic impulsion at all. I remember as an illustration of the saving power of this definite connection, a tale told me by a distinguished labor leader in England. His affections had been starved, even as a child, for he knew nothing of his parents, his earliest memories being associated with a wretched old woman who took the most casual care of him. When he was nine years old he ran away to sea and for the next seven years led the rough life of a dock laborer, until he became much interested in a little crippled boy, who by the death of his father had been left solitary on a freight boat. My English friend promptly adopted the child as his own and all the questionings of life centered about his young protégé. He was constantly driven to attend evening meetings where he heard discussed those social conditions which bear so hard upon the weak and sick. The crippled boy lived until he was fifteen and by that time the regeneration of his foster father was complete, the young docker was committed for life to the bettering of social conditions. It is doubtful whether any abstract moral appeal could have reached such a roving nature. Certainly no attempt to incite his ambition would have succeeded. Only a pull upon his deepest sympathies and affections, his desire to protect and cherish a weaker thing, could possibly have stimulated him and connected him with the forces making for moral and social progress.

This, of course, has ever been the task of religion, to make the sense of obligation personal, to touch morality with enthusiasm, to bathe the world in affection—and on all sides we are challenging the teachers of religion to perform this task for the youth of the city.

For thousands of years definite religious instruction has been given by authorized agents to the youth of all nations, emphasized through tribal ceremonials, the assumption of the Roman toga, the Barmitzvah of the Jews, the First Communion of thousands of children in Catholic Europe, the Sunday Schools of even the least formal of the evangelical sects. It is as if men had always felt that this expanding period of human life must be seized upon for spiritual ends, that the tender tissue and newly awakened emotions must be made the repository for the historic ideals and dogmas which are, after all, the most precious possessions of the race. How has it come about that so many of the city youth are not given their share in our common inheritance of life's

best goods? Why are their tender feet so often
ensnared even when they are going about
youth's legitimate business? One would sup-
pose that in such an age as ours moral teachers
would be put upon their mettle, that moral
authority would be forced to speak with no
uncertain sound if only to be heard above the
din of machinery and the roar of industrialism; that it would have exerted itself as never
before to convince the youth of the reality of
the spiritual life. Affrighted as the moralists
must be by the sudden new emphasis placed
upon wealth, despairing of the older men and
women who are already caught by its rewards,
one would say that they would have seized
upon the multitude of young people whose
minds are busied with issues which lie beyond
the portals of life, as the only resource which
might save the city from the fate of those who
perish through lack of vision.

Yet because this inheritance has not been
attached to conduct, the youth of Jewish birth
may have been taught that prophets and
statesmen for three thousand years declared
Jehovah to be a God of Justice who hated op-

pression and desired righteousness, but there is no real appeal to his spirit of moral adventure unless he is told that the most stirring attempts to translate justice into the modern social order have been inaugurated and carried forward by men of his own race, and that until he joins in the contemporary manifestations of that attempt he is recreant to his highest traditions and obligations.

The Christian youth may have been taught that man's heartbreaking adventure to find justice in the order of the universe moved the God of Heaven himself to send a Mediator in order that the justice man craves and the mercy by which alone he can endure his weakness might be reconciled, but he will not make the doctrine his own until he reduces it to action and tries to translate the spirit of his Master into social terms.

The youth who calls himself an "Evolutionist"—it is rather hard to find a name for this youth, but there are thousands of him and a fine fellow he often is—has read of that struggle beginning with the earliest tribal effort to establish just relations between man and man, but he still needs to be told that after all justice can only be worked out upon this earth by those who will not tolerate a wrong to the feeblest member of the community, and that it will become a social force only in proportion as men steadfastly strive to establish it.

If these young people who are subjected to varied religious instruction are also stirred to action, or rather, if the instruction is given validity because it is attached to conduct, then it may be comparatively easy to bring about certain social reforms so sorely needed in our industrial cities. We are at times obliged to admit, however, that both the school and the church have failed to perform this office, and are indicted by the young people themselves. Thousands of young people in every great city are either frankly hedonistic, or are vainly attempting to work out for themselves a satisfactory code of morals. They cast about in all directions for the clue which shall connect their loftiest hopes with their actual living.

Several years ago a committee of lads came to see me in order to complain of a certain high school principal because "He never talks to us about life." When urged to make a clearer statement, they added, "He never asks us what we are going to be; we can't get a word out of him, excepting lessons and keeping quiet in the halls."

Of the dozens of young women who have begged me to make a connection for them between their dreams of social usefulness and their actual living, I recall one of the many whom I had sent back to her clergyman, returning with this remark: "His only suggestion was that I should be responsible every Sunday for fresh flowers upon the altar. I did that when I was fifteen and liked it then, but when you have come back from college and are twenty-two years old, it doesn't quite fit in with the vigorous efforts you have been told are necessary in order to make our social relations more Christian."

All of us forget how very early we are in the experiment of founding self-government in this trying climate of America, and that we are making the experiment in the most materialistic period of all history, having as our court of last appeal against that materialism only the wonderful and inexplicable instinct for justice which resides in the hearts of men,—which is never so irresistible as when the heart is young. We may cultivate this most precious possession, or we may disregard it. We may listen to the young voices rising clear above the roar of industrialism and the prudent councils of commerce, or we may become hypnotized by the sudden new emphasis placed upon wealth and power, and forget the supremacy of spiritual forces in men's affairs. It is as if we ignored a wistful, over-confident creature who walked through our city streets calling out, "I am the spirit of Youth! With me, all things are possible!" We fail to understand what he wants or even to see his doings, although his acts are pregnant with meaning, and we may either translate them into a sordid chronicle of petty vice or turn them into a solemn school for civic righteousness.

We may either smother the divine fire of youth or we may feed it. We may either stand stupidly staring as it sinks into a murky fire of crime and flares into the intermittent blaze of folly or we may tend it into a lambent flame with power to make clean and bright our dingy city streets.

DATE DUE

APR 1 8 1997			
NOV 0 6 1997			
MAR 1 5 1998			
GAYLORD			PRINTED IN U.S.A.